The Cuban Economy in a New Era
An Agenda for Change toward Durable Development

Edited by Jorge I. Domínguez, Omar Everleny Pérez Villanueva,
and Lorena G. Barberia

Translated by Dick Cluster

Published by Harvard University David Rockefeller Center for
Latin American Studies

Distributed by Harvard University Press
Cambridge, Massachusetts
London, England
2017

Publisher's Cataloging-In-Publication Data

Names: Domínguez, Jorge I., 1945– editor. | Pérez Villanueva, Omar Everleny, edi-
    tor. | Barberia, Lorena, 1971– editor. | Cluster, Dick, 1947– translator.
Title: The Cuban economy in a new era : an agenda for change toward durable
    development / edited by Jorge I. Domínguez, Omar Everleny Pérez Villan-
    ueva, and Lorena Barberia ; translated by Dick Cluster.
Other Titles: David Rockefeller Center series on Latin American studies, Harvard
    University.
Description: [Cambridge, Massachusetts] : Harvard University David Rockefeller
    Center for Latin American Studies, 2017. | Cambridge, Massachusetts ; Lon-
    don, England : Harvard University Press, 2017. | Series: The David Rockefeller
    Center series on Latin American studies, Harvard University | Includes bibli-
    ographical references.
Identifiers: ISBN 9780674980358
Subjects: LCSH: Cuba—Economic conditions—21st century. | Economic devel-
    opment—Cuba—History—21st century. | Cuba—Politics and government
    —21st century.
Classification: LCC HC152.5 .C83 2017 | DDC 330.97291—dc23

Contents

List of Figures

List of Tables

List of Acronyms

BANDEC	Banco de Crédito y Comercio
BCC	Banco Central de Cuba
BM	Banco Metropolitano
BPA	Banco Popular de Ahorro
CADECA	Casas de Cambio
CAF	Corporación Andina de Fomento
CCS	Cooperativas de Crédito y Servicio
CEEC	Centro de Estudios de la Economía Cubana
CIEI	Centro de Investigaciones de la Economía Internacional
CEPAL	Comisión Económica para América Latina y el Caribe
CMEA	Council on Mutual Economic Assistance
CNA	Cooperativas No-Agropecuarias
CPA	Cooperativas de Producción Agropecuaria
CUC	Pesos cubano convertibles
CUP	Pesos cubanos
DFI	Direct foreign investment
EURODAD	Red Europea sobre Deuda y Desarrollo
FLACSO	Facultad Latinoamericana de Ciencias Sociales
GATT	General Agreement on Tariffs and Trade
GDP	Gross Domestic Product
IDB	Inter-American Development Bank
IBRD	International Bank for Reconstruction and Development
IDA	International Development Association
IFI	International Financial Institutions

IMF   International Monetary Fund

OAS   Organization of American States

ONEI   Organización Nacional de Estadística e Información

PCC   Partido Comunista de Cuba

MINCIN   Ministerio de Comercio Interior

MPYMES   Micro, Pequeñas, y Medianas Empresas

PYMES   Pequeñas y Medianas Empresas

SDR   Special Drawing Rights

TCP   Trabajo por cuenta propia

UBPC   Unidad Básica de Producción Cooperativa

WTO   World Trade Organization

List of Contributors

Lorena G. Barberia is an Associate Professor in the Department of Political Science at the University of São Paulo. Her primary research and teaching interests are political economy, comparative politics, and political methodology. Much of her recent work is aimed at analyzing redistributive politics in Latin America. She is also a research associate at the David Rockefeller Center for Latin American Studies at Harvard University. Her publications include three previous co-edited books published through the Harvard University David Rockefeller Center for Latin American Studies and Harvard University Press, *The Cuban Economy at the Start of the Twenty-First Century*, ed. J.I. Domínguez, O.E. Pérez Villanueva and L. Barberia (2004); *Cuban Economic and Social Development: Policy Reforms and Challenges in the 21st. Century*, ed. J.I. Domínguez, O.E. Pérez Villanueva, M. Espina Prieto and L. Barberia (2012); and *Social Policies and Decentralization in Cuba: Change in the Context of 21st Century Latin America*, ed. J.I. Domínguez, M. Zabala Argüelles, M. Espina Prieto, and L. Barberia.

Humberto Blanco Rosales is a full professor at the Center for the Study of the Cuban Economy at the University of Havana. He has been a visiting scholar in universities in the United States, Canada and Mexico. His research focuses on management and innovation.

Dick Cluster is a writer, translator, and former Associate Director of the University Honors Program at the University of Massachusetts at Boston. He is co-author, with Rafael Hernández, of *History of Havana* (Palgrave-Macmillan, 2006). His translations of Cuban fiction include novels by Mylene Fernández Pintado and Abel Prieto, story collections by Pedro de Jesús and Aida Bahr, and the anthology *CUBANA: Contemporary Fiction by Cuban Women* (with Cindy Schuster). Scholarly and other nonfiction translations include books from Cuba, Mexico, Colombia, and Spain. His most recent publication is a new anthology of Latin American baseball fiction, *Kill the Ámpaya*, that was published in 2017 by Mandel Vilar Press.

Ileana Díaz Fernández is a full professor at the Center for the Study of the Cuban Economy at the University of Havana. She is the principal investigator of a project on innovation and entrepreneurship and coordinates a research center on entrepreneurism studies at the University of Havana. She has been a visiting scholar at Columbia University and her three books have received prizes from the Cuban Academy of Sciences.

Jorge I. Domínguez is the Antonio Madero Professor for the Study of Government and former vice provost for international affairs at Harvard University. He has been president of the Latin American Studies Association. His work includes three previous co-edited books published through the Harvard University David Rockefeller Center for Latin American Studies and Harvard University Press, *The Cuban Economy at the Start of the Twenty-First Century*, ed. J.I. Domínguez, O.E. Pérez Villanueva and L. Barberia (2004); *Cuban Economic and Social Development: Policy Reforms and Challenges in the 21st. Century*, ed. J.I. Domínguez, O.E. Pérez Villanueva, M. Espina Prieto and L. Barberia (2012); and *Social Policies and Decentralization in Cuba: Change in the Context of 21st Century Latin America*, ed. J.I. Domínguez, M. Zabala Argüelles, M. Espina Prieto, and L. Barberia.

Oscar Fernández Estrada is a full professor at the School of Economics at the University of Havana (UH) and President of the Cuban Society for Planning and Prospective Studies (ANEC). From 2011 to 2016, he was Adviser for the Commission for the Implementation and Development of Reform, headed by the Vice-President of the Council of Ministries of Cuba. From 2014 to 2016, he was Director of the Center for Studies of Public Administration at the Superior School of Government Officers. He was also the Founder-Director of the Planning and Statistics Office at the University of Havana, and the Head of the Department of National Economy Planning at the School of Economics at UH. He has also served as a Consultant to ECLAC (CEPAL) on economic planning. He has published more than twenty articles and book chapters on the Cuban economy, and has been a lecturer and visiting scholar at several international universities.

Orlando Gutiérrez Castillo is a professor at the Center for the Study of the Cuban Economy at the University of Havana. He has also been a faculty member at the School of Accounting and Management at the Universidad Autónoma de Coahuila since 2015. He has coordinated international projects with Canada and Venezuela. His publications include chapters in 21 books and two of his articles were awarded prizes by the Cuban Academy of Sciences in 1999 and 2014.

Jessica León Mundul is an assistant professor at the Center for the Study of the Cuban Economy at the University of Havana. Her research focuses on macroeconomic policy with a focus on monetary policy. She has been a visiting researcher at the David Rockefeller Center for Latin American Studies at Harvard University and the School of Economics at the Universidad de Barcelona. Her current dissertation for her doctoral thesis focuses on Cuba's public debt and its impact on monetary stability. She also coordinates the undergraduate training program of the University of Havana and the Cuban Central Bank.

Dayrelis Ojeda Suris is an assistant professor at the Center for the Study of the Cuban Economy at the University of Havana. She is the editor of the *Boletín Semestral del CEEC (Centro de Estudios de la Economía Cubana)* and is a member of the Cuban Scientific Society of Cooperatives (*Sociedad Científica Cubana de Cooperativismo*) and the *Red de Cooperativas* at the University of Havana. She is the author of several publications on public finance, knowledge management, internal controls and cooperatives in Cuba. She has also served as an advisor and a consultant to several enterprises and cooperatives.

David J. Pajón Espina is an assistant professor at the University of Havana. He has served as a trade specialist at the Korea Trade-Investment Promotion Agency (KOTRA) in Havana, where he coordinated the Knowledge Sharing Programme) and advised on macroeconomic issues. His research includes work on health tourism and credit policy in Cuba. He also works as an entrepreneur in the tourist sector in Cuba.

Omar Everleny Pérez Villanueva is a full professor and a former director of the Center for the Study of the Cuban Economy (*Centro de Estudios de la Economía Cubana*) at the University of Havana. With Jorge I. Domínguez and Lorena G. Barberia, he edited *The Cuban Economy at the Start of the Twenty-First Century* (Harvard University Press, David Rockefeller Center for Latin American Studies, 2004). With Jorge I. Domínguez, Mayra Espina Prieto and Lorena G. Barberia, he edited *Cuban Economic and Social Development: Policy Reforms and Challenges in the 21st. Century* (Harvard University Press, David Rockefeller Center for Latin American Studies, 2012). He has also served as an adviser to the Government of the City of Havana, a visiting professor and scholar at universities including Columbia University, the Institut des Hautes Etudes de l'Amérique Latine (IHEAL) at the Université Sorbonne Nouvelle, and a visiting researcher at the Institute of Developing Economies, Japan External Trade Organization (IDE-JETRO) in Japan. He was a visiting researcher at the David Rockefeller Center for Latin American Studies at Harvard University in 2004 and 2010.

Marlén Sánchez Gutiérrez is a full professor at the Center for Research (*Centro de Investigaciones*) of the University of Havana. Her research focuses on international finance. She is the author of one book, several chapters and articles on finance for development, international financial architecture, and external debt. She was a manager for research at the Cuban Central Bank and worked as a consultant to international organizations. She has presented her research in various countries including the United States, Spain, Switzerland, Denmark, South Korea, Japan, France, Morocco, Mexico, China, Venezuela, Trinidad and Tobago, Haiti, the Dominican Republic, Bolivia and Ecuador.

Ricardo Torres is an associate professor with the Centro de Estudios de la Economía Cubana (CEEC) at the University of Havana. He was a Japanese government scholar at Hitotsubashi University in Japan (2007–2009) and visiting researcher at Harvard University (2011), Columbia University (2013) and American University (2015). He has participated in conferences and courses in universities and research centers in several countries in Latin America, Europe, Asia, Africa and the United States and has published several articles in international journals and books. Among his most recent publications are "Policies for Economic Growth: Cuba's New Era" in *Cuba's Economic Change in Comparative Perspective* (Washington, D.C.: Brookings Institution, 2014), "No More Free Lunch: Reflections on the Cuban Economic Reform Process and Challenges for Transformation" (Springer, New York, 2014), "Inversión y asignación de recursos: una discusión del caso Cubano" (*Cuban Studies Journal* 44, 2016), "Economic transformations in Cuba: a review" (*Third World Quarterly*, 2016) and "Vicinity Matters: Cuba's Reforms in Comparative Perspective" (*International Journal of Cuban Studies*, 2016).

1

Cuba's Economy at the End of Raúl Castro's Presidency: Challenges, Changes, Critiques, and Choices for the Future

Jorge I. Domínguez

Challenges

In December 2016 Cuba's former president, Fidel Castro, died, and in that month Cuba's National Assembly learned that gross domestic product fell by 0.9 percent during 2016, well below what the government had expected the previous December. It was Cuba's first acknowledged outright recession since 1993. Earlier that summer, President Raúl Castro gave several reasons for the economic setback; the most notable was Venezuela's inability to deliver petroleum products to Cuba and, consequently, Venezuela's weakened ability to pay for service and other imports from Cuba (Castro 2016).

This transparent recognition that the relationship with Venezuela was at the core of Cuba's new economic problems signaled publicly the end of the economic "model" fashioned by the late presidents Fidel Castro and Hugo Chávez at the start of the twenty-first century. That relationship featured an exchange of Venezuela's petroleum principally for Cuba's service exports, above all in health care services but also across social, economic, political, and military arenas. Those politically negotiated bilateral trades had led to an economic mini-boom in Cuba, with the growth rate of gross domestic product accelerating every year from two percent in 2002 to twelve percent in 2006. Subsequently this relationship faltered; the growth rate declined every year down to 1.4 percent in 2009 (Pérez Villanueva 2012a, 22). As Ricardo Torres' chapter in this book shows, since 2009 the growth rate of gross domestic product has been modest, well below Cuba's performance during the 1971–1985 period, another time of excellent relations with another external supporter, the Soviet Union. The public recognition of the withering of the Venezuelan economic relationship occurred only in 2016.

Yet the economic and economic policy problems that President Raúl Castro inherited went beyond the effects on Cuba of Venezuela's economic and political tribulations. When Raúl Castro became Cuba's acting president in August 2006, the following legacies characterized Cuba's economy:

- Technologically obsolete manufacturing, especially since the collapse of the Soviet Union in the early 1990s;
- A bankrupt sugar industry, whose output had exceeded 8.1 million metric tons per year at the end of the 1980s but had fallen below 2.0 million metric tons by the 2005–2006 harvest, Fidel Castro's last as president, and remained below that level every subsequent year (ONEI 2015: Table 9.5);
- Stagnant agriculture and dependence on food imports, requiring $775 million worth of agricultural imports from the United States during the last five years of Fidel Castro's presidency (computed from U.S. International Trade Administration 2015);
- Very high volatility in economic growth rates, as noted above;
- The global 2008–2009 economic crisis, the world's worst since the 1930s, with adverse impacts on several of Cuba's main international partners, especially on Venezuela, on which Cuba depended disproportionately, but also on the European Union and Brazil. Among many factors, these effects contributed to Cuba's decision to suspend international payments on its economic obligations; in fact it was a general financial default.

The aim of this book is to examine Cuba's economic performance and policies under Raúl Castro to the end of 2016, focusing on specific topics that bear especially on the process of policy change. This is the fourth and most recent publication in this century from a team of scholars that has included Cuban economists, Harvard University scholars, and colleagues at a few other institutions, all dedicated to examine Cuba's economic circumstances and economic policies. The first two were books (Domínguez, Pérez Villanueva, and Barberia 2004; Domínguez, Pérez Villanueva, Espina Prieto, and Barberia 2012), and the third was a special dossier in the refereed journal *Cuban Studies* (2016). The books have been published by Harvard University's David Rockefeller Center for Latin American Studies, distributed by Harvard University Press.[1]

Here I introduce the themes of the book, drawing on the insights and analyses of my fellow authors,[2] remaining deeply in debt to them; I am solely responsible, however, for any mistakes of fact or interpretation. Having already posed some of the difficult challenges that the Cuban economy has encountered, I turn next to identify some of the salient policies that the Cuban government has adopted to accelerate economic growth. Thereafter, I illustrate the public debate on the wisdom of some of these policies, as evidenced, perhaps surprisingly, on the website of the official Communist Party newspaper. Then I turn to the diagnostic and prescriptive analyses presented in the rest of the book, followed by a brief conclusion.

Changes: What Policies Did Cuba's Government Adopt to Improve Economic Growth?

President Raúl Castro inherited the very difficult economic circumstances summarized above, as well as a set of economic policies and institutions that seemed incapable of accelerating Cuba's low rate of economic growth. But he also inherited some important market-oriented policy changes first adopted under President Fidel Castro's leadership. In particular, these are the welcome to foreign direct investment, principally through joint ventures between foreign firms and Cuban state enterprises, the opening to international tourism, and the encouragement of remittances from the Cuban diaspora worldwide but especially from those residing in the United States. As already noted, in this century's first decade Cuba and the United States also agreed on a program whereby the United States exported agricultural products to Cuba.

One promising early policy change—the authorization of foreign direct investment—has been greatly constrained in its effects on Cuba, however. Cuba publishes little information on such investment. The number of joint ventures with foreign direct investment in Cuba increased rapidly from 1990 to 2002, but it then fell precipitously in the closing years of Fidel Castro's presidency, through 2008 (Pérez Villanueva 2012b: 216). The dates matter. Cuba's relationship with Venezuela took off in 2003, and its spike may have rendered Cuban officials less interested in promoting foreign direct investment. The annual flow of foreign direct investment into Cuba as a proportion of gross domestic product has been 0.5 percent, Latin America's lowest and lower than that for emerging economies in East Asia (Torres 2016: 55). Cuba's opening of a special economic zone at the port of Mariel was designed to lure foreign investors, but three years after its opening it had fewer than ten foreign firms operating there; the government's bureaucratic requirements have deflated what may some day be a valuable initiative. Outside mining and hotels, the positive impact of foreign investment remains modest.

From its start, the Raúl Castro presidency launched a wide variety of discrete economic policy changes. Although limited in scope, they have moved in approximately the same direction, consistently, and without significant reversals. The first welcome policy change was to economize on the time of Cubans, reducing the number of officially sponsored mass demonstrations and rallies to a few national holidays, thereby saving time for production and for leisure.

President Raúl Castro's next significant policy change was announced in 2008. Idle land would be given in usufruct to those ready to cultivate it. However, the state retained the ownership of the land, and the right to cultivate it was limited to a ten-year term, albeit renewable. The duration was the same independent of the crop, which discouraged investment in perennial crops whose economic return requires a longer time horizon. Moreover, at the end of the period, the rights holder would be obligated to turn over the investments he made to the state, which would pay compensation at its discretion, but no compensation would be paid for dwellings, on the assumption that the agricultural producer would live in town and commute to the countryside (Nova 2013: 57–60). Cuba's statistical yearbook reported 1,233 thousand hectares of idle land in 2007 and still 962 thousand hectares of idle land in 2014 (ONEI 2012: Tables 9.2 and 9.3; ONEI 2015: Table 9.2). The slow pace of implementation provoked an exasperated President Raúl Castro, at the Sixth Congress of the Communist Party of Cuba held in April 2011, to complain that, although nearly four years had elapsed since the policy change, "there remain thousands and thousands of hectares of agricultural lands awaiting" willing cultivators, recalling that Cuba had continued to import expensive agricultural products (Castro 2011). Agricultural output in 1997 constant prices grew only by a cumulative 7 percent from 2009 to 2014, a pitifully modest annual increase (computed from ONEI 2015: Table 5.7). The agricultural policy change had been excessively constrained; these poor results demonstrate it.

The longest-lasting policy undertaking was the preparatory effort, begun soon after Raúl Castro became Cuba's president in February 2008 (he served as acting president from August 2006 until then), that culminated in the September 2010 announcement (in Spanish, the *Lineamientos*) of a new set of policies for the Cuban economy, described modestly as an "updating" of economic policies. The *Lineamientos* were formally authorized by the Sixth Communist Party Congress in April 2011 (Sexto Congreso 2011).

A noteworthy change was the reactivation of a policy first authorized in the 1990s under President Fidel Castro, but now made wider and more flexible, to permit Cubans to opt for self-employment. As Pérez Villanueva notes in his chapter, such self-employment was authorized in 1994, with approximately 121,000 licenses, reaching a peak in 2005 with 165,000 licenses, declining significantly thereafter. The policy authorized in 2010 increased the number of permissible categories for self-employment from a base of 157 to 201 in 2012 and, crucially, permitted the self-employed license holder to hire employees (not merely relatives), pay them a salary, and obtain credit for business operations. By 2015, the number of self-employment licenses exceeded half a million and, counting cooperative members and private farmers, the number of people in the private sector in 2014 well exceeded a million people (ONEI 2015: Table 7.2) out of Cuba's population of 11.2 million people. In effect, this meant that small businesses have been authorized, albeit under remaining constraints; I return to this topic below.

These private sector policy changes have been successful. One indirect measure is tax contribution. Taxes on profits (including the profits of foreign direct investors) increased 42 percent from 2009 to 2014, and personal income taxes for those years jumped 172 percent (calculated from ONEI 2015: Table 6.3). The personal income tax falls principally on the self-employment sector, although it also includes taxes paid by musicians, artists, and athletes as well as bonuses paid in some state enterprises; in any event, the higher income of all of these has been produced as a result of economic policy liberalizations, and thus it is a reasonable indicator for overall private sector policy changes (for discussion of tax policy, Pons Pérez 2016).

Raúl Castro's most salient policy change turned out more effective than he had surmised soon after he announced it. In October 2010, the government stated its intention to cut state employment because it had an excessive or "inflated" number of employees, reporting that 500,000 state employees would have to look for new jobs "in the next few months" ("Proteger . . . 2010). The then-Minister of Economy and Planning Marino Murillo was exact, indicating "a reduction of state employees (some 497 thousand)" (Murillo 2010), with a corresponding increase in the number of jobs in the non-state sector (the approved label to describe the private sector). Two months after Murillo's precise numbering, Raúl Castro publicly indicated that the "inflated" worker rolls could not be reduced by any "inflexible" deadlines ("Sesionó . . ." 2011), thereby draining urgency from this process. Nevertheless, the number of state employees did drop by nearly 423,000 from 2010 to 2011 (ONEI 2012: Table 7.2), coming close to matching Murillo's numerical target. From 2011 to 2014, the number of state employees fell cumulatively by an additional 552,000 (calculated from ONEI 2015: Table 7.2).

The most impressive economic policy accomplishment of Raúl Castro's presidency has been the successful renegotiation of Cuba's international debt obligations, as Torres and Sánchez Gutiérrez note in their chapters. Cuba emerged from the 2008–2009 financial crisis having defaulted across the board on its financial obligations to official and private creditors, many of the latter being trade financing debts. Cuba had been in default since 1986 on its convertible-currency international debts (Domínguez 1989: 211–217); this old debt had never been renegotiated. Following the collapse of the Soviet Union, Cuba refused to recognize a legacy debt to the Russian Federation. In that context, the debt renegotiation results in the second decade of this century have been impressive. Cuba has successfully renegotiated its debt with the Russian Federation. Many of the unpaid trade credits (and imports payments for which Cuba had fallen into arrears) were owed to China; there was also a successful Sino-Cuban debt agreement. Most strikingly, in December 2015 Cuba reached agreement with the Paris Club, the set of official creditors on the old debt on which Cuba had defaulted in 1986 and on subsequent trade credits. Cuba has signed renegotiation agreements with individual governments within the Paris Club as well as others. These renegotiations involved significant debt forgiveness, but each also required of Cuba to start to service the newly recognized extant debt. This agreement reopened Cuba's access to international financing, but of course it also imposed a new debt service obligation at a time when the Cuban economy was not growing much.

In short, Cuba has adopted various economic policy changes along with other smaller adjustments. But the results remain meager, even for the most successful change, namely, private-sector small-business growth. The international debt renegotiations hold promise for future financing but impose a short-term burden. The economy's performance remains weak ten years after Raúl Castro became Cuba's acting president and then president. The direction of the reforms has been clear, cumulative, and in the judgment of this book's authors, apt and appropriate. The challenge is how to accelerate economic change to harvest better economic outcomes.

Critiques: Social Discontent

Both the process of change and the dearth of results have nurtured a low-key social discontent. People have started to question and, at times, to criticize the economic policies implemented during the period of so-called economic updating, begun informally in Fall 2010. There are various sources of evidence for this social grumbling, but I deliberately choose only three examples published by *Granma*, the Communist Party's official newspaper, on its website. The newspaper need not endorse these views, but it has clearly endorsed their incorporation into the public debate. This is a tribute to a greater tolerance for critical views, but it also likely indicates that some of these critical views have sufficient support within the Communist Party that its official newspaper is permitted and encouraged to publish them. If grumbling exists at this high level, then take notice.

The first example focuses on the wider inequality observed in Cuban society. This implies a critique of some of the consequences of the economic policy changes. The second example voices sharp criticism regarding the insufficiencies and arbitrariness of the foreign investment policy. The implication of this critique is that the state should undo the policies that the public considers wrong-headed in order to accelerate the process of change on a sounder footing. And the third example concerns a debate that links economic considerations and the role of Cubans abroad. Most public views on this third topic support further changes, but there is a greater division of opinion on this matter than on the previous two, where the commentaries had indicated a consensus in the criticism.

As the new economic policy has encouraged the development of high-fashion women's dresses for exports, in September 2016 *Granma* published a glossy article displaying a photograph of seven women wearing elegant dresses. Linda commented that the dresses were beautiful, but "what are the prices?" Sara added "but I imagine that an ordinary Cuban woman like me will not even reach the store where they will be sold, given that these will be prices for tourists and not for Cubans who earn a living through a salary." Lisbecita concurred, also on the same day, doubting that "ordinary Cubans such as us" could ever afford them (Alberdi Benítez 2016). These public comments are expressions of concern regarding inequality of opportunities and inequalities of result in the context of a society where differences in income and standard of living had been modest until the end of the 1980s (Espina Prieto and Togores González 2012). They are cautionary words for economic policy changes as they imply the need for greater attentiveness to the burden of inequality (for a substantive discussion of the problem of inequality, see Zabala, Echevarría, Muñoz, and Fundora 2015).

A second area of discontent developed as the new economic policy sought to promote foreign direct investment. In April 2014, *Granma* published the text of the new law (Law 118) that promotes and regulates such investment, amending Cuba's previous law on foreign investment. *Granma* also permitted online commentary. Cuban regulations require foreign firms operating in Cuba to hire their Cuban employees through a state organization acting like a hiring-hall monopoly. Reynaldo criticized this procedure because, he wrote, the state retained twenty percent of the salary and applied an exchange rate between the foreign currency and the Cuban currency that was half what market rates would indicate. Pedro objected to the same procedure, which in his view risked favoritism, privilege-granting, and needless bureaucracy; he favored free and direct contracting between the firm and the employee. Eduardo chastised the new policy because it prohibited partnerships between a foreign firm and Cuba's emerging private sector authorized under self-employment regulations. Someone else, self-titled "Yo Mismo," chided the Mariel special economic zone project by arguing that such facilities should exist throughout Cuba (Asamblea Nacional del Poder Popular 2014).

In December 2014, the debate reappeared in the *Granma* online commentaries because the pertinent regulations to implement the foreign investment law had just been issued. This time the emphasis was almost exclusively on the burden on each worker from the tax and foreign exchange policies embedded in the new law. Alex, Alejandro, Paco, and Roche, among others, analyzed the arithmetic in the law, concluding that a Cuban employee would receive only between 7 to 10 percent of what a foreign firm pays the Cuban state hiring-hall monopoly. Paco labeled this state monopoly a "parasite" ("Nuevas . . ." 2014). *Granma* did not prevent the publication of these views or seek to contradict them.

On the next day, *Granma* convened three officials for an online forum to discuss the new foreign investment regulations that bear on payments to Cuban employees. The officials did not dispute the calculations presented by the online critics; they limited themselves to emphasize that the new payments scheme was far more favorable to Cuban employees than the previous one. In this exchange, Jose L observes that the state retains 91.5 percent of the firm's pay, commenting "I've not seen anything like it anywhere in the world or in past Cuban history." Someone who signs as ATG asks rhetorically, "do you think this is correct???" [*sic*], then writes that it is excessive. Iris is tougher. A Cuban worker, she argues, is being discriminated against in her own country and equates the policy to "theft." Humberto insists that the firm and the employee should be free to enter into a contract with no role for the intermediary state enterprise; otherwise, this is "state exploitation of the worker and this is not what we revolutionaries have defended with so much sacrifice." Carlos deems the participation of these officials at this online forum a "disaster" because they cannot "explain the reasons for these regulations" ("Funcionarios . . ." 2014). This critique of the intrusive and seemingly arbitrary role of the state in regulating an otherwise private contract between a joint venture firm and an employee shows significant resentment toward those policies, seen as predatory and unjustified.

A third example of social discontent was triggered on the pages of *Granma* by an article that analyzed why Cuba had been performing less well in international sports competitions in recent years than in the past. The occasion was the 2015 Pan American Games in Toronto, where, for the first time since 1971, Cuba had dropped out of the top two spots for medal counts, finishing in fourth place. The author, Oscar Sánchez Cerra, stated that people were unhappy with this outcome because finishing in one of the top two spots had been publicly identified as a Cuban objective for these Games. Sánchez Cerra provides explanations for these outcomes, but I focus on the commentary from readers. Pedro notes that foreign trainers are no longer hired to prepare the Cuban athletes, presumably for lack of funds to pay them. Luis complains that Cuban trainers and athletes lack "free and systematic" Internet access to enable them to keep up with trends and athletes in other countries. Reyner argues that Cuban sports could be financially self-sufficient upon signing international contracts and investing the gains in sustaining sports in Cuba. Rey supports "free contracting for our athletes" and discarding the policies that penalize those who go abroad to earn income yet are willing to return regularly to Cuba for sports participation. Alberto demurs, however, insisting that athletes who are "deserters" should reimburse Cuba for their training costs ("Panamericanos . . . 2015).

All three examples illustrate different forms of social discontent, ranging from concerns about inequality that stem from the new economic policies, to government labor market policies and taxation seen as unacceptably predatory, to policies that constrain Cuban athletes and disappoint their fans. The comments show more disagreement on how to deal with Cuban athletes who leave the country, and probably most agreement on the unfairness of the state monopoly hiring hall. In every respect, however, these are serious questions about the new economic policies. Rigid policies regarding sports come in for criticism, but so does a policy that rests on inequality of access to expensive clothes. Considerable fury is aimed at the new policy governing the labor market for joint venture enterprises, which is perceived as unfair by long-existing Cuban social standards for failing to reward and compensate Cuban workers. On the screens of the Communist

Party's official newspaper, there is a strong demand for change, albeit in no case for a return to past economic policies or standing still.

Choices for the Future: What Is to Be Done?

Lenin's classic question applies to the prospects of political action; I invoke it because economic policy changes require leadership within the party and the government. In this section, I summarize the diagnosis of a problem discussed in each of the chapters and indicate the authors' recommendations for a more productive future.

Macroeconomic performance. Cuba's economic performance matters to each of this book's authors. Ricardo Torres opens his chapter with a gripping discussion of the persistent and in some cases worsening deficiencies of that performance. These deficiencies linger or worsen despite various government efforts to improve the results. Torres notes that one key factor in the sustained deceleration of the economic growth rate since 2008 was that Cuba's service exports had not diversified into sufficient markets, depending excessively just on Venezuela's. Another was Cuba's 2009 default on its international financial obligations, which constrained its already limited access to financial markets. Cuba's commodity exports have remained limited, not showing significant growth paths. The government adopted a tough austerity program but deferred attempts to unify its multiple exchange rate policies and, in fact, added new exchange rate levels depending on the sector of the economy. Torres highlights the serious distortions that this exchange rate policy generates and the threat it poses to Cuba's growth prospects. One effect of the exchange rate policy on the labor market is that professionals switch from working in the professions for which they were trained, but in jobs where they are woefully underpaid, to jobs that require little education but pay more: a tourist taxi driver earns more than a mechanical engineer.[3] Torres also reports some policy successes. Cuba has successfully renegotiated its international debts and resumed service payments. Through 2016, it had stabilized the budget deficit and controlled inflation, although the planned countercyclical policies adopted for 2017 will widen the budget deficit significantly.

Among important policy changes is the restructuring of property rights, permitting the growth of the private sector (self-employment, farmers, and cooperatives, this last one showing the slower growth). At the same time, Torres observes that the centralized allocation of resources stumbles for various reasons, one of them the difficulty of obtaining sufficient information to operate effectively. Foreign investment flows remain limited while remittances remain important since the early 1990s.

Finally, Torres examines the documents that outline the Communist Party's priorities for the next fifteen years, adopted at its April 2016 Seventh Communist Party Congress. He agrees with the diagnosis that calls attention to technological backwardness, under-implemented existing policies, foreign exchange bottlenecks, and infrastructure deficiencies, in addition to the noted distortion of labor market incentives and a rise in corruption. He emphasizes key steps toward the future, all of which require shifting more quickly and effectively from decisions already made to their implementation:

- Unify the exchange rate;
- Dismantle the regulatory obstacles to foreign investment inflows;
- Authorize and establish wholesale markets to supply the private sector;
- Permit Cuban workers greater choice of employers;
- Develop a market for Republic of Cuba bonds to finance projects and the budget.

Planning. Revolutionary Cuba's foundational institutional design in the early 1960s featured a commitment to governmental planning of the economy. Oscar Fernández Estrada's chapter describes the key elements of the initial design, the changes introduced in planning structures and policies over time, and the challenges to state planning that showed up from the beginning. From the 1960s to the 1980s, planning decisively replaced the market as the instrument to allocate resources; that outcome was consistent with what was broadly believed during those years in Cuba to be required under socialist theory.

Cuba instantly faced two challenges, which were prevalent throughout those years but, more importantly, are inherent to any highly centralized and mandatory planning process such as took place in various Eastern European countries before 1990. One problem has been the relatively weak and persistently insufficient statistical base, which then and ever since, in Cuba and in communist Europe, made it more difficult to implement a central planning scheme that necessarily required abundant and precise statistics. The other was to rely on physical output, and hence material balances, and to forego financial statistics as a principal means to allocate resources; this made it more difficult to assess costs or gains. Cuba adopted a material-balances approach in part by emulating the practice in then-communist Europe, and firmed it up especially in the 1970s as an instrument for coordination through the Council for Mutual Economic Assistance (CMEA), which grouped the Soviet Union and Eastern European countries; Cuba joined it early in that decade. This approach, more understandable in that earlier period, became especially inappropriate for Cuba upon the CMEA's collapse in the early 1990s. It has become a mental-framework obstacle to a more effective Cuban economic policy, given how internationally open Cuba's economy has become.

Under the shock of the collapse of the Soviet Union and the rest of communist Europe, Cuba refashioned its planning system to rely more on financial statistics and relevant decisions, while retaining a secondary role for material balances as a consideration for resource allocation. Since the 1990s, market considerations have played a larger role in Cuba's planning processes, but the external constraints (fewer external resources available than before 1990) and a brief Venezuela-induced growth respite in the early years of the twenty-first century have continued to distort resource allocation.

Fernández Estrada argues that the Cuban government has recognized the necessity of changing the planning process and its methods to focus on regulated markets as key allocators of economic resources. There is a lag, however, in implementing the adjustment that is in part caused by the residual impact of the mental framework that once privileged the non-financial material-balances approach. It is also caused in part by the severe distortions in Cuba's economy as a result of the multiple exchange-rate regime, which is of course all the more reason to change the planning process. Fernández Estrada recommends, therefore, that Cuba's planning process should:

- Focus on long-term development objectives instead of its most common practice to address short-term economic bottlenecks.
- Accept the role of regulated markets in Cuba's contemporary economy and incorporate market mechanisms into the government's own planning processes.
- Drop the mentality of the non-financial material-balances approach.
- Shift from mandatory central commands to indirect means of market regulation, relying on financial considerations in the allocation of resources.
- Shift from a preference for monopoly or oligopoly products and services markets to promote competition between enterprises in the state and non-state sectors in order to promote efficiencies, improve quality, and better serve clients.

Small and medium-sized private firms. Cuba's most successful economic reform has been the opening to private activities that form small and medium-sized businesses. Omar Everleny Pérez Villanueva observes in his chapter that such businesses are key sources of growth in many of the world's economies, just as they often are the principal sources of job creation. Moreover, small businesses had been numerous in Cuba before the revolution and had been key generators of jobs. Access to labor, capital, and good management is essential to small and medium-sized businesses; their success is predicated, of course, on the state not preventing them from such resources.

Pérez Villanueva documents how extensive had been the development of such small and medium-sized firms in Cuba in the 1950s outside of the sugar industry, a process that would end by the late 1960s. Very large state enterprises took their place, emphasizing vertical integration at the expense of inter-firm coordination, impeding competition while hoarding and under-utilizing resources, thereby generating idle capacity. In the early 1990s, Cuba began to adopt a variety of economic policy changes, among them the authorization of self-employment in 1993. The constraints and limitations on the self-employed (example: a private restaurant could only have twelve chairs) undermined their growth potential and impeded job creation; the impediments also provided multiple incentives to violate the regulations, seeding illegality.

President Raúl Castro's decision in 2010 to permit an expansion of the self-employed sector opened the door for economic growth and job creation. The number of licenses to operate in this private sector skyrocketed over the next half-decade. At the 2016 Seventh Communist Party Congress, Raúl Castro said that the expression "self-employment" obscured the reality: these were micro, small, and medium-sized businesses. He urged a rhetorical recognition of this new reality. Pérez Villanueva concurs. He observes that this private sector is already rich in human resources and portends a more efficient use of other economic resources. For these reasons, Pérez Villanueva emphasizes specific suggestions to better establish the role of such firms in Cuba's economy:

- Recognize them as enterprises under corporate law, not just self-employment. This formal change would authorize the micro-, small-, and medium-sized private businesses to open bank accounts to receive and make payments, accumulate profits and savings, receive credits, and pay taxes, none of which has been hitherto possible. All of it would likely reduce illegal behavior and improve government tax collection. It would make it easier for these private firms to operate, grow, seek new opportunities, and enter into partnerships.

- Authorize a wholesale market to supply the private sector, thereby reducing the price premium incurred by obtaining such supplies in illegal markets and hence greatly fostering market and firm efficiencies.
- Enable this private sector to obtain access to credit, with less paperwork and without demanding a level of collateral assets for small loans that private businesses (best considered start-ups) do not yet possess.
- Permit micro, small, and medium-sized businesses, as corporations, to export and import. This, too, would contribute to efficiencies because firms would obtain the inputs that they require, and only those, and their successes would thus contribute to Cuba's international earnings.

Non-agricultural cooperatives. One Cuban policy experiment from this century's second decade has been the authorization of non-agricultural and services cooperatives. Dayrelis Ojeda Suris examines this topic. She first describes the long trajectory of the development of cooperatives in Cuba since 1960 and writes that the two types of private agricultural cooperatives in existence were economically much more profitable at the start of the severe economic crisis in the early 1990s than were the state enterprises. This superior early performance of private cooperatives helps to explain why since the early 1990s government policies tilted to authorize new forms of cooperatives. Her focus, however, is on the decision incorporated in April 2011 in the *Lineamientos*, as approved by the Sixth Communist Party Congress, to authorize non-agricultural cooperatives, for which regulations were first issued in 2012.

Ojeda Suris notes the extraordinary complexity of the approval process for new non-agricultural cooperatives. It is a multiple-veto system, which can delay and paralyze the process at the municipal or provincial level or at the level of the conglomerate of state enterprises in the sector where the cooperative is expected to operate; the establishment of even a simple non-agricultural cooperative requires the approval of the Council of Ministers. This complexity maximizes incentives to delay or stop the approval process and hence generates much uncertainty. In practice, moreover, three-quarters of the non-agricultural cooperatives approved and in operation have been established because a state enterprise wished to divest itself of such activities; in fact it was a process of partial privatization initiated by the state. Other means of cooperatives creation have either not been authorized or have been seriously constrained. All of the non-agricultural cooperatives in operation were approved in 2013 and 2014, but none since then; over half are just in Havana. Proposals to create other such cooperatives have been pending. Non-agricultural cooperatives have been approved principally for the restaurant, retail trade, and construction sectors, areas where state enterprises had typically been inefficient; the cooperatives, however, may have inherited the same inefficiencies.

Ojeda Suris finds that the non-agricultural cooperatives in operation have been working well. They meet objectives, and improve productivity and efficiency as well as the income of cooperative members. The cooperative members believe that they are the joint owners of their cooperative and govern it democratically. They work together to improve the cooperative's performance. She finds, however, as do other authors in this book, that the lack of wholesale markets to provide the necessary inputs is a serious impediment to the proper functioning of these cooperatives, as is also the myopic behavior and policies of the Cuban banking sector toward these cooperatives. Ojeda Suris recommendations include:

- Streamline and accelerate the process of approval of new cooperatives;
- Permit them to import necessary inputs, given the lack of wholesale marketing options, and to export to improve their financing;
- Push implementation of the law that also authorizes the creation of second-level cooperatives, that is, cooperatives of cooperatives in order to improve shared access to finance, purchases and sales, comprehensive training opportunities, and management services.

Financing the non-state sector. What should be the scope of non-state forms of production (self-employment, cooperatives, and individual farmers) and how should they be financed? Jessica León Mundul and David Pajón Espina worry that these non-state entities have yet to be authorized to import their necessities directly; if or when they are authorized to import, then their next challenge is how to finance those imports or other investments to develop their activity. For their analysis, they focus on the self-employed who are already in a category akin to small and medium-sized firms, and examine the extraordinarily limited scope of financing and the burdensome financing mechanisms available since the policy was authorized in late 2011.

León Mundul and Pajón Espina note that under the policy terms the non-state sector cannot be granted credits in convertible currency. To be sure, the self-employed may obtain personal credits in Cuban pesos, go to a lawful state foreign-exchange entity to exchange their pesos into dollars, and then pay a premium for the additional transaction costs. Even the Cuban-peso loans, whose minimum worth was set at $120 (if they were convertible into U.S. dollars), were considerably restricted in the 2011 regulations. Loan-term duration was initially set at 18 months at variable interest rates but, more dauntingly, the borrower had to demonstrate that the business had been in operation and thus be in a position to pledge collateral assets to secure the loan; by definition, this regulation ruled out financing start-ups. Subsequently, the amount of minimum eligible loans dropped to $50 in U.S. dollar equivalents, terms were lengthened, and a wider array of possible items became eligible for collateral (family jewelry, for example). Non-agricultural cooperatives were explicitly included as eligible for loans.

The effects of this credit policy are noteworthy but not surprising. By the end of 2013, only 550 loans had been granted to the more than 440,000 self-employed. Most credits granted have gone not to the self-employed but to private farmers, and some to non-agricultural cooperatives. There has been a disconnect, these authors observe, between the growth of self-employment and the growth of credit for private borrowers. They worry that there has been a bias in favor of financing non-agricultural cooperatives because these were originally "born" out of state enterprises, not because these cooperatives present better proposals than the self-employed. Moreover, the highly intrusive set of procedures that the banks have imposed on any potential borrower is an additional disincentive for the self-employed to seek loans.

León Mundul and Pajón Espina argue, therefore, that important changes should be adopted:

- Design regulations to permit the financing of start-ups, dismantling the obstacles that impede such financing.
- Evaluate projects according to their merits, not according to the type of property owners (e.g., self-employed or cooperative).
- Choose developmental criteria to govern decisions regarding credit allocation.
- Make it possible for the state to share risks while awarding loans to projects that meet national goals.
- Authorize the self-employed to incorporate in order to be able to import and export.

State enterprise autonomy and innovation. Cuba's economic challenges require that all enterprises, including state enterprises, be well managed and capable of innovation. Ileana Díaz Fernández, Humberto Blanco Rosales, and Orlando Gutiérrez Castillo focus on the microeconomic issues that foster or impede the process of innovation. They emphasize enterprise strategy, capacities, and incentives for cooperation as they bear on the likelihood of the generation and application of innovations. They observe that government policy has rendered Cuba's state enterprises uniformly large, has frequently changed the oversight procedures for enterprises thus affecting their operations, and has emphasized low-level, simple practical problem-solving that lacks wider use or applicability. At the close of 2014, 151 state enterprises showed operating financial deficits, a significant number in the Cuban economy.

Díaz, Blanco, and Gutiérrez observe that even the 2014 regulation designed to foster economic change and apply it to state enterprises featured rules for the micromanagement of firms, a near-uniformity of expectations regardless of the type of firm, reliance on extensive documentation and standard guidebooks for routine decisions, and failure to reconcile the multiple demands that entities external to a state enterprise place on its operations. The state enterprise is, in effect, the lowest rung of a bureaucratic ladder; given the complexity, it might as well be run by lawyers who can discern the regulations, not by managers who should seek profitability and efficiency. None of the state requirements implies that client satisfaction should be a key to performance; therefore, nine out of ten enterprises have little information about their clients. The plan is rigid, seeks minute regulation through paperwork, and discourages creativity, for which some margin of autonomy is essential.

Research in Cuba shows that although innovation is a buzzword frequently mentioned in regulations, priority is always accorded to short-term over long-term investments and to operations over investments. The requirement to demonstrate that the enterprise has a strategy may be as simple as producing a piece of paper saying so. Nearly nine out of ten enterprises report that the pressure to fulfill the annual plan trumps any support for innovation that goes beyond such immediacies. Innovation, therefore, is poorly rewarded. Access to international information regarding the "state of the field" for the appropriate technologies is very limited. The modest innovation initiatives are poorly integrated throughout the enterprise and have scattered impact. Personnel training for innovation is also extremely limited; enterprises nearly unanimously report that they lack financing for innovation, notwithstanding the evidence of obsolescing equipment, deferred maintenance, and breakdowns of machinery and equipment.

Díaz, Blanco, and Gutiérrez note that Cuba's long-term hopes and plans seem to depend on the generation, application, and diffusion of innovation. They recommend, therefore, that:

- State enterprises be accorded much greater autonomy from the ministries and other central agencies to design and implement their strategies and manage their operations;
- To foster such independence the state should authorize and encourage state enterprises to invest in innovation, especially investments in the quality of their personnel to prepare for more creative undertakings;
- Managers of state enterprises should be accorded incentives and rewards to propel them in this direction.

Multilateral financing sources. Cuba applied tough adjustment processes to cope with the effects of the 2008–2009 worldwide economic crisis and ever since, with the decline of the economic capacity of its principal partner, Venezuela. Because it had defaulted on its international financial obligations, it tightened the economy for the most part on its own resources. Marlén Sánchez Gutiérrez asks whether Cuba may successfully seek support from international financial institutions (IFIs). Under Raúl Castro's presidency, Cuba's successful renegotiation of its international obligations within the framework of its agreement with the Paris Club makes it possible to think more broadly. Sánchez Gutiérrez examines first an array of obstacles that have stood in the way, and still make it difficult, for Cuba to access such IFI financing.

One long-standing obstacle has been U.S. government opposition to Cuban membership in the International Monetary Fund (IMF), the World Bank, or the Inter-American Development Bank (IDB). A second obstacle has come from those who support the socialist character of Cuba's economy and believe that it is incompatible with membership in such IFIs, but other socialist countries such as China and Vietnam have already joined these IFIs, thereby mitigating the weight of this objection. If both of these obstacles are removed, or greatly weaken, then Cuba may have the option to join the IFIs. Should it?

Sánchez Gutiérrez emphasizes the near-universal membership in such organizations and the great practical utility of having their support for Cuba to access international markets. The IMF would assist Cuba in coping with its balance of payments imbalances, while the World Bank would support development projects in Cuba. She notes, however, two difficulties. One is the requirement for Cuba's national accounts to apply IFI standards and for such statistical information to become transparent; in the past, for national security reasons, Cuba's national accounts have been opaque. Another is the requirement to adopt appropriate exchange rate policies. However, these problems may vanish. For its own reasons, Cuba may choose policies of greater transparency; it is already committed to exchange rate unification, although it has had enormous difficulty in making the change—a change for which the IFIs would provide support. Cuba would likely resist, however, the kind of financial monitoring that is also a routine procedure for IMF grantees. Above all, the author indicates, accepting IMF conditionality on its loans is the most likely obstacle to a changed Cuban-IMF relationship. Sánchez Gutiérrez intelligently notes, however, that there is a margin for maneuver and negotiation between any country and the IMF, which may assuage Cuban government concerns. (World Bank membership requires prior membership in the IMF.)

Sánchez Gutiérrez also considers possible Cuban membership in the IDB, where Cuba could be more comfortable with discussion in Spanish, the widespread Latin American membership, and the regional focus. Beyond the obstacles still posed by U.S. policy, IDB membership also requires the activation of membership in the Organization of American States and acceptance of its definition of "democratic political regime." The Cuban government is unlikely to take such a step in the near term.

In all such IFIs, one important advantage of membership is that they provide access to technical training and advice, which Cuba has long sought. Its officials could adopt and adapt as they wish, benefiting from learning while at the same time applying their own criteria for their choices. China and Vietnam have employed these technical services extensively as a benefit of their membership in the IMF and the World Bank, and they have borrowed considerable funds from the latter. Consequently, Sánchez Gutiérrez considers that Cuba should:

- Actively explore the possibility of relationships with the IFIs.
- Be cognizant of the differences between the IFIs and the need to exercise conscious choice and discretion in accessing their financial resources.
- Be especially attentive to the array of technical services that the IFIs would make available as a matter of course.
- Make it one of its priorities in negotiations with the United States to insist that the U.S. government eliminate its opposition to the possibility of Cuban access to the IFIs. Relations with the United States became more challenging under the Trump administration, however.

Conclusion

As this book is published, Cuba reaches the scheduled end of Raúl Castro's presidency in February 2018, still trying to cope with the effects of the crisis of 2008–2009; the decline in Venezuela's capacities as Cuba's main economic partner; the dysfunctions from an inherited structure that had bankrupted the sugar industry and permitted widespread deferred maintenance and technological obsolescence; sustained stagnation principally but not exclusively in agriculture; and an approach to decision making, from the factory to the national government, whose top three priorities have been caution, caution, and caution.

The commitment to economic policy change has been reiterated time and again. President Raúl Castro has emphasized his goal of a prosperous and sustainable socialism, and the two Communist Party congresses under his leadership have endorsed a path to change. The pattern of application of the announced changes has been remarkably slow, however, and by the government's own measures most initiatives have not been implemented in full, even though most were first formally authorized in 2010–2011. Cuba's potential for change may also dim if the Trump administration in fact curtails U.S. travel to Cuba because this will impair the growth potential of the nascent private sector that has gained from such travelers.

Cuba's first new leadership following the retirement of Raúl Castro must decide whether to speed implementation of economic policy changes, consistent with the decision to open and deregulate the economy sufficiently to accelerate economic growth, fund social policies, and improve the people's standard of living.

Notes

1. There is significant high-quality scholarly literature on the Cuban economy published outside Cuba. In this chapter, however, I focus on scholarly works published by Cuban authors who live and work in Cuba, in part to highlight their work, and in part to make it clear that the analyses and recommendations summarized in this chapter come from such authors, not from authors abroad.
2. Several authors in this book have been affiliated at one point with the University of Havana's Centro de Estudios de la Economía Cubana (CEEC). The CEEC's edited books deserve mention for their quality and also because some work published there overlaps with work published in this book. In particular, see the series of books called *Miradas a la economía cubana*, of which the most pertinent for this book is Pérez Villanueva and Torres Pérez 2015.
3. These are not abstract examples. I have personally met such persons.

Bibliography

Alberdi Benítez, Virginia. 2016. "Tríada en el arte y la moda." *Granma*, August 31, http://www.granma.cu/cultura/2016-08-31/triada-en-el-arte-y-la-moda, accessed, September 5, 2016.

Castro, Raúl. 2016. "El pueblo revolucionario cubano nuevamente se crecerá." *Granma*, July 9, http://www.granma.cu/cuba/2016-07-08/el-pueblo-revolucionario-cubano-nuevamente-se-crecera, accessed September 5, 2016.

Castro, Raúl. 2011. *Granma*, April 20, http://www.granma.cu/secciones/6to-congreso-pcc/artic-23.html, accessed April 20, 2011.

Cuban Studies. 2016. Volume 44.

Domínguez, Jorge I., Omar Everleny Pérez Villanueva, and Lorena Barberia. 2004. *The Cuban Economy at the Start of the Twenty-First Century*. Cambridge, MA: Harvard University David Rockefeller Center for Latin American Studies and Harvard University Press.

Domínguez, Jorge I., and Omar Everleny Pérez Villanueva, Mayra Espina Prieto, and Lorena Barberia. 2012. *Cuban Economic and Social Development: Policy Reforms and Challenges in the 21st. Century*. Cambridge, MA: Harvard University David Rockefeller Center for Latin American Studies and Harvard University Press.

Domínguez, Jorge I. 1989. *To Make a World Safe for Revolution: Cuba's Foreign Policy*. Cambridge, MA: Harvard University Press.

Espina Prieto, Mayra, and Viviana Togores González. 2012. "Structural Change and Routes of Social Mobility in Today's Cuba: Patterns, Profiles, and Subjectivities." In *Cuban Economic and Social Development: Policy Reforms and Challenges in the 21st Century*, ed. Jorge I. Domínguez, Omar Everleny Pérez Villanueva, Mayra Espina Prieto, and Lorena Barberia. Cambridge, MA: David Rockefeller Center for Latin American Studies and Harvard University Press.

"Funcionarios aclaran dudas sobre pago a trabajadores vinculados con la inversión extranjera." 2014. *Granma*, December 16, http:///.granma.cu/cuba/2014-12-16/funcionarios-aclaran-dudas-sobre-pago-a-trabajadores-vinculados-con-la-inversion-extranjera, accessed December 17, 2014.

Murillo, Marino. 2010. *Granma*, December 19, http://www.granma.cubaweb.cu/2010/12/19/nacional/artic 12.html, accessed December 19, 2010.

Nova, Armando. 2013. *El modelo agrícola y los lineamientos de la política económica y social en Cuba*. Havana: Editorial de Ciencias Sociales.

"Nuevas disposiciones sobre pago a trabajadores vinculados con la inversión extranjera." 2014. *Granma*, December 15, http://www.granma.cu/cuba/2014-12-15/nuevas-disposiciones-sobre-pago-a-trabajadores-vinculados-con-la-inversion-extranjera, accessed December 16, 2014.

ONEI (Organización Nacional de Estadística e Información). 2015. *Anuario estadístico de Cuba, 2014*, http://www.onei.cu/aec2014/09%20Agricultura%20Ganaderia.pdf, accessed September 25, 2016.

_____. *Anuario estadístico de Cuba, 2011*, http://www.onei.cu, accessed August 29, 2014.

"Panamericanos, Toronto, 2015." 2015. *Granma*, July 26, http://www.granma/cu/panamericanos-toronto-2015/2015-07-26/detras-de-toronto-y-sus-medallas, accessed July 28, 2015.

Pérez Villanueva, Omar Everleny. 2012a. "The Cuban Economy: An Evaluation and Proposals for Necessary Policy Changes." In *Cuban Economic and Social Development: Policy Reforms and Challenges in the 21st Century*, ed. Jorge I. Domínguez, Omar Everleny Pérez Villanueva, Mayra Espina Prieto, and Lorena Barberia. Cambridge, MA: David Rockefeller Center for Latin American Studies and Harvard University Press.

_____.2012b. "Foreign Direct Investment in China, Vietnam, and Cuba: Pertinent Experiences for Cuba." In *Cuban Economic and Social Development: Policy Reforms and Challenges in the 21st Century*, ed. Jorge I. Domínguez, Omar Everleny Pérez Villanueva, Mayra Espina Prieto, and Lorena Barberia. Cambridge, MA: David Rockefeller Center for Latin American Studies and Harvard University Press.

Pérez Villanueva, Omar Everleny, and Ricardo Torres Pérez. 2015. *Miradas a la economía cubana. Análisis del sector no estatal*. Havana: Editorial Caminos.

Pons Pérez, Saira. 2016. "Balance de cuatro años de reformas en el sistema tributario cubano." *Cuban Studies* 44: 66–89.

"Proteger al trabajador disponible pero sin recargar económicamente al Estado." *Granma*, October 27, 2010, http://www.granma.cubaweb.cu/2010/10/27/nacional/artic 02.html.

"Sesionó reunión ampliada del Consejo de Ministros," *Granma*, March 1, 2011, http://www.granma.cubaweb.cu/2011/03/01/nacional/artic06.html, accessed March 1, 2011.

Sexto Congreso del Partido Comunista de Cuba. 2011. *Información sobre el resultado del debate de los Lineamientos de la Política Económica y Social del Partido y la Revolución*. Havana.

"Texto de la Ley No. 118 de la Inversión Extranjera." 2014. *Granma*, April 16, 2014, http://www.granma.cu/cuba/2014-04-16/asamblea-nacional-del-poder-popular, accessed April 21, 2014.

Torres, Ricardo. 2016. "Inversión y asignación de recursos: Una discusión del caso cubano." *Cuban Studies* 44: 43–65.

U.S. International Trade Administration, U.S. Department of Commerce, http://tse.export.gov, accessed August 12, 2015.

Zabala, María del Carmen, and Dayma Echevarría, Marta Muñoz, and Geydis Fundora. 2015. *Retos para la equidad social en el proceso de actualización del modelo económico cubano*. Havana: Editorial Ciencias Sociales.

2

An Analysis of the Cuban Economic Reform

Ricardo Torres

Cuba's singular trajectory over the past fifty-five years has included momentous recent events. In its first three decades, the Cuban revolutionaries set ambitious social goals, counting on significant support from the Soviet Union and the Council for Mutual Economic Aid (CMEA). Since 1990, the sudden change in outside economic and political conditions put many of the most important conquests of Cuban society to the test. Until recently, it was hard to devise any clear strategy for maintaining a robust condition of well-being in such an adverse context, and particularly a strategy for overcoming the economic crisis engulfing the country. The measures adopted in the 1990s were presented as temporary and, in general, did not face the fact that the world had changed and so had the aspirations and conceptions of development.

For many, the coming of the administration of Raúl Castro represented a watershed. Immediately after he assumed the presidency, ideas were put forward that later became instrumental in a historic change in the Cuban socioeconomic model. The declared objective was to achieve a level of economic performance sufficient to support the great aspirations for ultimate social well-being and social justice that most Cubans share. However, in the medium term the means to achieve those goals can actually act to their detriment, as has occurred with social equity. Meanwhile, the world continued to change, and nations faced new obstacles and opportunities.

The challenge to reach the desired objectives is almost overwhelming. At the end of the 1980s, however, Cuba could demonstrate social achievements that often matched those of developed countries. Even today, after a very difficult period, the rates of infant mortality, life expectancy, and average years of education are among the best in the world. There have also been outstanding results in sports, the arts, and special needs education, access to a universal system of social security, and certain guarantees for low-income people. In such areas as housing, water and sewer

systems, public transportation, broad access to information and communications technology, and productive jobs, the advances have been much
more modest.

All of these areas have been weakened to some degree by the economic crisis of the past twenty years. A certain decline in the quality
of health care and education has been noted (González 2011); results
in international sports competitions have deteriorated since the start of
the twenty-first century. Deterioration has accumulated in the housing
stock,[1] and a substantial income gap among different strata of the population is beginning to be observed (Ferriol 2004, Espina 2012). These
setbacks can be explained to a degree by the difficult economic conditions of the past years, but at the same time, many of the problems in
the functioning of the socioeconomic system are not new; clear symp-
toms of exhaustion of the model of economic growth could be seen
from mid-1980 onward (Triana 1999, Figueras 1999). For five and a half
decades, the economic achievements that allowed for continuation and
improvement of the social indicators have been much less impressive. Per
capita income is lower than in many countries of Latin America that have
inferior social indicators (Torres 2014).

This picture set off alarms at the highest levels of government, warning
that the nation was pursuing an unsustainable trajectory with important
consequences for its economic, political, and social model. Since Raúl Castro announced the need to introduce "structural changes," government
actions can be described as following two main tracks: the correction of
macroeconomic disequilibria, and implementation of the program set
forth in the Guidelines,[2] the Conceptualization,[3] and the National Development Plan 2030[4] that point to a new socioeconomic model.

In this chapter I discuss the fundamental facets of the transformations
since 2007 in both areas, stressing their main limitations and challenges.
The chapter has six main sections. Following this introduction, the next
two sections review economy-wide performance and results. The next section is an analysis of the transformations introduced in key aspects of the
economic model, following which is a critical discussion of the proposals
set forth in the nine documents approved at the April 2016 Seventh Congress of the Communist Party. The chapter closes with a review of key
aspects considered in the light of Cuba's economic development challenges.

Overall Economic Performance

Since its first days, the Raúl Castro administration confronted a complex
macroeconomic situation. In 2009–2010, the economy faced a financial

crisis, and more recently, it has had to struggle with the problems of several of its most important trading partners (Venezuela, Russia, and Brazil).

Beyond strictly economic measures, even before the April 2011 Sixth Congress of the Communist Party, the introduction of changes with broad impact on daily life was under way. In 2008, Cuban citizens were allowed to acquire cellular phones and stay in tourist hotels; 2009 brought new access to the Internet, followed by liberalization of the purchase of construction materials in 2011, new opening to foreign travel in 2013, and new customs regulations on importing foreign goods in 2014. President Barack Obama's initiatives in 2009 and 2011 (easing restrictions on visits and the sending of remittances by relatives residing in the U.S., as well as broadening other U.S. residents' access to travel to Cuba for academic, cultural, or religious reasons), the packages of newly loosened U.S. regulations since 2014, and the reestablishment of diplomatic relations in June 2015—all contributed to consolidation of a sense of irreversible change, although that change seems more precarious under the Trump administration.

From an economic point of view, the Guidelines approved in 2011 sought to eliminate barriers to economic growth and to create conditions for sustained growth in GDP that would allow for a qualitative leap in the level of development. It was said that economic growth needed to stabilize at a rate above 5 percent. That would require sustained growth in productive investment, progressive relaxation of foreign-imposed strangulation, and a transformation of the economic structure that would promote productivity gains in excess of real wages. This scenario would generate increased competitiveness and, in turn, import substitution and better conditions for unification of the dual currency.

Despite important transformations that did occur, the general economic performance has not significantly improved, while some disequilibria have sharpened. A look at some general indicators helps to understand the context of recent years.

The rate of GDP growth slowed notably since 2008. This stemmed from a combination of three adverse factors. The first was the economic slowdown already evident in 2007 resulting from declines in the growth rate of the sale of professional services to Venezuela,[5] which had been the fundamental source of expansion in the 2004–2007 period. The main cause was the saturation of that market, in which levels of imported Cuban services were already very high and demand could not continue growing as fast as in the initial years. Moreover, the drop in world petroleum prices also reduced Venezuela's capacity to purchase such Cuban services. Though these results could be foreseen, the development of new

Table 2.1: Selected Cuban Macroeconomic Indicators, 2007–2016 (Annual Average Growth Rates, Percent)*

	2007	2008	2009	2010	2011	2012	2013	2014	2015	2016
GDP (constant 1997 prices)	7.3	4.1	1.4	2.4	2.7	3.0	2.7	1.0	4.3	-0.9
Consumer Price Index **	1.8	-0.1	-0.1	1.6	3.6	2.0	0.6	2.1	2.8	–
Unemployment rate (%)	1.8	1.6	1.7	2.5	3.2	4.6	3.3	2.7	2.4	2.0
Investment (constant prices)	-3.5	51.3	–19.0	-3.8	2.2	6.0	12.9	-8.9	24.9	10.2
Gross capital formation (% of GDP)	10.2	14.8	10.9	10.1	8.5	8.6	9.4	7.6	9.4	–
Exports of goods and services (current prices)	20.7	4.9	–14.9	31.1	20.7	8.8	-0.4	-4.2	– 16.1	–11.2
Imports of goods and services (current prices)	6.0	43.3	–35.4	18.7	29.8	-0.6	4.8	–11.1	-9.2	-0.01
Balance of goods and services (millions of dollars)	1,559.3	–1,735.5	1,245.5	3,119	2,240	3,771	2,991	3,947	2,350	–48.6
Budget surplus or deficit (% of GDP)	-3.2	-6.9	-4.9	-3.6	-3.8	-3.8	-1.2	-2.2	- 5.8	-6.8

Sources: Author's estimates based on data from ONEI various years and UNCTAD (2017).
Notes: * except as otherwise indicated; ** includes only prices denominated in CUP.

markets of similar size was unlikely, given the particular conditions of the Venezuelan market.

The second rate decline stemmed from the impact of the world financial crisis on the Cuban economy, beyond the already noted drop in the oil price, which affected Venezuelan purchases. Economic problems beset the majority of countries in the world, severely affecting the prices of some of Cuba's most important products such as nickel, and diminishing the flow of international visitors. Nickel prices dropped from a high of a little more than $50,000 per ton in April 2007 to $9,600 in December 2009, a drop of 80 percent of its value. These changes were immediately reflected in revenue from exports. Nickel sales were the leading element in foreign sales of goods, and the third most important foreign exchange earner, after professional services and tourism. The third setback was the disruption of the tourism market because of economic problems in Cuba's major tourist supply markets, Europe and Canada; tourism gross revenues dropped compared to 2008.

All this provoked a difficult situation in the evolution of Cuba's balance of payments, sharpened by a substantial increase in imports starting in late 2008 to deal with needs stemming from the damage caused by three severe hurricanes that hit Cuba that year. Added to that were high prices for food, fuel, and other key imports, which caused a significant increase in that year's outlays.

This unfavorable evolution was directly reflected in the growth of the country's foreign debt and, therefore, in the volume of resources devoted to honoring commitments to providers and creditors (although this deficit situation was already under way, tied to large investments in energy and transportation). The new troubles made it difficult to meet these commitments, which led to a partial suspension of payments, most critically in the period 2009–2010. Some writers (Mesa-Lago and Vidal 2009) estimate that difficulties in access to foreign financing meant economic damage equivalent to 4 percent of GDP while export volumes reduced expected growth rates by another 2.9%. The only mitigating factor in 2009 was that exchange rates slightly (0.5 percent) lessened the negative impact on GDP growth.

To confront this situation, the government implemented an adjustment program aimed at resuming payments of international debts. The severest impact was on imports, which dropped by more than a third in 2009; since then, their volume has depended on the availability of foreign financing.[6] This abrupt decline affected quite a few lines of production, as is typical in a country extremely dependent on foreign purchases for its manufacturing cycle and whose import coefficient has grown in this century because its domestic industrial base has decayed. In this sense, although reducing imports was necessary, the measure contributed significantly to reduce the economy's growth in recent years.

In contrast to the past, this time the restructuring did address the problem of the foreign debt and of improving the country's very poor reputation as a credit risk. Recent years have seen substantial reductions in the foreign debt thanks to long-term bilateral debt renegotiation with major creditors such as Japan, Russia,[7] Mexico, and China. In all cases, Cuba has obtained cancellation of at least 70% of the bilateral debt and rescheduling of future payments with acceptable conditions. In December 2015, an accord was reached with the ad hoc Paris Club[8] group for a definitive solution to Cuba's debts, which had amounted to more than $11.1 billion, of which 76 percent were forgiven and the rest rescheduled over an eighteen-year period. Still unresolved is the debt with the London Club,[9] estimated by one creditor[10] at about $6.48 billion.

The other component of the adjustment had to do with investments, which display a highly cyclical pattern. Table 2.1 shows that they dropped significantly in 2009 and 2010, beginning a slight recovery thereafter. For 2016, another contraction in this indicator was foreseen as part of an adjustment related to balance of payments difficulties. Reduction in investment volume implies an immediate recessive effect on the economy, curtailing economic growth over the longer run, because new productive capacity is not installed nor is infrastructure extended and modernized. That trend reinforces a pattern that has lasted for almost twenty years.

An increased state budget deficit in 2008 led to the adoption of a restrictive spending policy. The budget dropped in 2009 and 2010, allowing for a return to an acceptable level of deficit during a period when revenues did not display a favorable dynamic. Given that Cuba did not have a market for public debt, the entire state debt was monetized, with direct effects on price stability. Therefore the deficit is a variable carefully monitored by the Central Bank. Any disequilibrium in this indicator should be corrected quickly so as to maintain low interest rates and stabilize the exchange rate in the CADECAs (state-run exchange booths), another variable to which the population's consumption level is very sensitive.

By 2017, the situation had modified slightly. Since 2015 the Cuban government decided to issue sovereign bonds in the domestic market to finance up to 70 percent of the public deficit. State-owned commercial banks buy these bonds at a set interest rate of 2.5 percent annually. This change provides more room for the government to use fiscal policies more actively because in the short term it effectively de-links the size of the fiscal deficit from price stability. During 2016–2017 there was a spike in the deficit, as the government sought to counter the economic recession. However, the growing public debt might be entering an unsustainable path that requires close monitoring. Furthermore, in supply-constrained economies, the impact of aggregate demand on production is very limited.

The priorities established in the Guidelines include a substantial shift in the fundamental allocation of investments: "Investments should be directed in prioritized fashion to the productive sphere and to services so as to generate short-term benefits, as well as to infrastructure investment needed for the sustainable development of the country's economy."[11] In terms of economic policy goals, economic growth and increased investment are central objectives over the medium and long terms. In Cuba's case, this could represent a notable change in the allocation of resources, given that the Cuban economy remains centrally planned.

Table 2.2: Composition or Structure of Value Added and Investments, by Large Sectors and Groups, Cuba (2010–2016), Percent

	2010	2011	2012	2013	2014	2015	2016
Value Added							
Goods	23.6	23.3	23.5	23.7	22.9	23.7	24.4
Infrastructure	10.3	10.3	10.6	10.7	11.0	11.2	11.7
Commercial services	29.0	29.8	30.6	30.7	31.4	31.9	32.7
Other services	37.1	36.6	35.3	34.9	34.6	33.3	32.6
Investment							
Goods	48.7	41.8	35.8	30.1	38.0	30.1	32.0
Infrastructure	20.7	17.1	27.1	28.6	19.8	23.3	22.3
Commercial services	19.7	25.4	24.1	26.7	28.1	32.6	33.3
Other services	10.9	15.6	13.0	14.5	14.2	14.0	12.4

Source: Constructed by the author from data in *Anuario estadístico de Cuba* (various years). Infrastructure includes electricity, gas, water; transport, warehousing, and communications, in accordance with the classification of the Sistema de Cuentas Nacionales.

Table 2.2 shows trends in value added and investments categorized by economic activity over a period of seven years. A new trend in value added is evident, one consonant with what the government has announced. Though growth rates are still modest, the increases took place mainly in goods and infrastructure. The latter gains show the greatest cumulative growth. This marks a shift from previous years, when social services led GDP growth, and it anticipates a progressive movement of the center of gravity toward material production and related (commercial) services.

In terms of investments, the picture is more mixed. Goods production remains low, although this assessment hides noteworthy increases in agriculture and the sugar industry. In infrastructure, the figures are highly influenced by the construction of the new port at Mariel, including the container terminal, railroads, and highways. Still, despite the attempt to break the vicious circle, investments maintain their cyclical behavior. In difficult periods, both investments and imports drop because it is impossible to take on debt, and they recover in the upswings of the cycle. Without functional insertion into international capital markets, this asynchronicity will persist. In 2016, faced with another complex scenario, a 17 percent drop in investments was announced as part of the readjustment of the plan for the year.

On the demand side, investment numbers are similar over the five years presented in Table 2.3, while net exports (balance of trade) fluctuated with a deteriorating trend that dramatically accentuated in 2016. The evidence in Table 2.3 confirms that investment throughout the period remained at about 13 percent, and the balance of trade at about 2.7 percent. Most significant is a slow but sustained gain of private consumption over public consumption. This is a change of great qualitative importance, stemming from the new directives related to the major equilibria. In a context of growing inequality, state spending that reaches all citizens equally through so-called "social consumption" has a much smaller effect on the perception of equity and in the mobilization of labor. The government hopes that increased private consumption, achieved through eventual improvement in real salaries in the public sector, can be more effective to recover the value of work and thus to increase productivity.

Table 2.3: Structure of Nominal GDP in Cuba (%)						
	2010	2011	2012	2013	2014	2015
Government consumption	35	35	32	32	32	32
Private consumption	50	53	54	54	55	56
Gross capital formation	11	8	9	9	8	9
Net exports (X-M)	4	3	5	4	5	3

Source: *Anuario Estadístico de Cuba* (various years)

The data do not allow for deeper investigation of this hypothesis, but in practice, it has been shadowed by various interrelated phenomena. For example, the delay in reforming state enterprises while obstacles continue facing the economy imply that the public sector will lag; compensation in the emerging private sector, and probably in the cooperative sector, has grown more rapidly. In turn, households continue receiving income from abroad via remittances, small-scale smuggling of goods to sell, and investments of a certain rentier slant such buildings. In this realm, differences among households are significant.

Macroeconomic Overview

To understand decision makers' priorities and their degrees of freedom to maneuver, it is of particular interest to discuss the essential characteristics and implications of the current monetary system, which is based on the circulation of two currencies and the use of multiple exchange rates. The system originated in the early 1990s within the framework of other anti-crisis measures. The main objective at that moment was to isolate the emerging sectors of the economy (tourism, foreign investment) from the risks of a devaluation associated with pressures on the official currency (the Cuban peso, CUP) that resulted from the enormous macroeconomic disequilibria accumulated between 1990 and 1994. This isolation made it possible to offer the necessary guarantees to investors about the value of the currency with which they would operate and the repatriation of their dividends. It also complemented other measures, such as the elimination of certain free services, higher prices on non-essential products, and the introduction of some taxes, all oriented toward controlling the state budget deficit, which reached 40 percent of GDP; controlling inflation; and restoring the value of the peso. These early goals were achieved in a relatively short time.

However, the persistence of this mechanism over twenty years created other problems, equally or more serious than those it originally intended to solve. Over time, many different markets have emerged, all operating simultaneously. Some function according to pricing mechanisms (regulated, fixed, or free-market), others use differing currencies (CUP, CUC, USD), and there are distinctions between formal and informal markets. Thus is it common for very similar goods and services to be exchanged at very different prices, which in turn feeds the growth of an informal market that arbitrages those price differences. Still more serious is the fact that both measurement of economic realities and price formation (including relative prices) are distorted by the lack of a unified, universal mechanism that reflects the relative scarcity of factors, inputs, and consumption goods. This leads inevitably to ineffective decision making on the part of producers, consumers, and the government itself, which needs that information to create the annual economic plan and forecast its evolution.

The most dangerous effects of this mechanism, however, are those that influence the dynamics of economic development. Differences in remuneration for different occupations cause a displacement of skilled workers toward positions that do not necessarily require high professional levels: e.g., a mechanical engineer drives a tourist taxi. For the individual, this can represent a short-term gain, but it can be a waste of resources at the societal level. It negatively affects the likelihood of increasing productivity over the medium term, worsens the current demographic picture (characterized by an eventual contraction and aging of the workforce[12]), and deprives the country of what all observers consider its major resource: a workforce with relatively high levels of qualification by the standards of a developing country.

In open economies, the exchange rate is a key price. It contributes to the allocation of resources toward marketable activities, which have a direct medium-term impact on the scarcity of hard currency, the essential source of the problem. The current monetary system feeds the inefficiency of a production sector that receives an implicit subsidy in terms of the few activities that can generate foreign currency surpluses. That is, the current dual currency and exchange system generates macroeconomic contradictions with perverse effects on measurement of productive activity and managing monetary policy. It also has negative effects on trends in the economic structure and productive potential, because it conspires against the development of sectors with saleable products and of various human-capital-intensive activities, two of the decisive areas for the nation's economic future.

Despite this disturbing element, an assessment of macroeconomic management reveals some important achievements. Inflation in the markets that operate in CUP continues to be under control, which in an environment of stagnation of nominal wages has contributed to limit the negative effect on real wages.[13] Nonetheless, the behavior of specific markets can vary significantly around this average. For example, food prices have shown a steadily rising trend, with an unfavorable impact on the populace. Additionally, there is a need to look at prices in CUC (the convertible peso)[14] about which there is no official data even though an important share of family consumption takes place in this currency.

In the midst of difficult conditions, a degree of order was restored in external finances, improving the country's financial position; credit, although limited in quantity, continues to enter the country. Import controls allowed for achieving surpluses in some years, though at the cost of reducing growth. Overall inflation and exchange rates have been stable.

There has been a reduction and then a stabilization of the budget deficit, with a reduction in the state's share of the economy.

Still, the net effect of these monetary policies contains a recessive bias: reduction of imports and investments; contraction of spending; restraining public sector wages, among other factors. Likewise, there is clearly much less progress in putting stimulus measures into practice, and those that have materialized lack coherence and depth. In the absence of this second component, macroeconomic stabilization is not sustainable. An analysis will be required about how to manage those disequilibria when the decision is made to move forward with currency and exchange rate unification.

Transformations in Key Areas of the Model through 2016

This section examines the fundamental elements of the program of long-term transformations, and to what degree these will contribute to make the macroeconomic adjustment achievements sustainable, as well as create new sources of lasting growth.

Property Structure

For fifty years, Cuba's economic model has demonstrated extreme caution about involving the private sector (and domestic capital especially) in productive activity. One of the distinctive characteristics of Cuba's institutional activity was the rapid transformation of the property structure inherited from the past. The deep economic crisis of the 1990s, however, highlighted a need to open the economy in order to increase efficiency; this included allowing new forms of property. This first great re-accommodation required a specific mandate from the 1991 Congress of the Communist Party and a constitutional reform from the National Assembly. What has been most controversial has not been the effort to attract foreign investment[15], but the opening of more room for the category called "self-employment."

The reforms in the property structure of land from 2007 onward, followed by the loosening of regulations governing "self-employment" in September 2010, and then the authorization of cooperatives outside the agricultural sector, combined to make the non-state sector in 2016 the largest since the early 1960s. Currently, 29 percent of the labor force works in that sector, more than at any time in past fifty years. To this figure must be added some employees officially tabulated as belonging to the state sector: those employed in mixed enterprises involving foreign capital, in offices representing foreign entities, and in fully foreign-owned businesses.

Table 2.4: Employment by Type of Property (Thousands)*

	2007	2016
Employed persons	4,867.7	4,591.1
State	4,036.1 (83%)	3,250.8 (71%)
Private	589.5 (12%)	1,139.2 (25%)
Small farmers**	451.1	540.8
Self-employed	138.4	598.4
Cooperative	242.1 (5%)	201.1 (4%)
Agriculture	242.1	189.8
Other sector	–	11.3

Source: (ONEI several years).

Notes: * In parentheses is their proportion as a percentage of total employment. ** Small farmers include those with usufruct tenure and the members of Credit and Service Cooperatives. The usufruct holders are not owners of the land; this is the category with the most growth since 2007 because of successive decrees authorizing usufruct distribution of idle land.

The figures reveal that the growth of the non-state sector is led by the greater number of private employees, with significant increases among both the "self-employed" and usufruct farmers. Non-agricultural cooperatives are also represented, though they still account for a small proportion of total employment. The process of creating these cooperatives is lengthy, and for completely new cooperative enterprises, it requires express approval by the Council of Ministers. A significant share of non-agricultural cooperatives comprises former state enterprises converted to this new form of management, which has generated some problems in operations and results (Piñero 2015). Their legal framework is still confusing because there is not yet a permanent body of legal regulations. The existing regulations contain weaknesses and contradictions that limit the full realization of the potential claimed for such cooperatives (Mesa 2015).

The structure of the data obscures other dimensions. Clearly, the informal economy and holding multiple jobs are common in the Cuban labor market. Individuals take note of wage and salary differences and allocate their time in order to maximize real income, but statistics based on reported numbers of employees do not reflect this allocation. In practice, they do not reflect what happens when a public sector employee devotes a number of hours a week to selling products imported as personal baggage. The categorization of this worker depends only on formal workplace rolls, while in terms of effective work hours and—more important—per hour earnings, he or she should be considered as employed in the informal economy. This matters because the statistics may significantly underestimate the role of the non-state sector and of market relationships in shaping individuals' preferences and work decisions, and thus distort the real effect of public employment policies.

Nevertheless, some aspects of the current process differ from previous transformations and make it qualitatively superior. The current modifications are taking place within a broader context of reforms in the economic model that also promote greater participation by foreign business and changes in management forms within Cuban state enterprises.[16] There is also discussion of real linkages between the state and non-state sectors through contracts for products and services. Additionally, new opportunities have been offered for access to the financial system through certain services and for obtaining credit, which in turn offers a number of challenges (León and Pajón 2015).

Resource Allocation Mechanisms

The mechanism for allocating resources is another element intrinsically linked to the essence of the Cuban model. Institutions fulfilling this function include the annual plan for the national economy, the state budget, the central state hard currency repository, and in fact the dual currency and exchange rate system itself.[17] Through these institutions, hard currency and inputs are allocated and capital accumulation is managed. This has been the institutional response to Cuba's inability to meet in full its own productive and social needs. The current form of that response assumes that a compatibility of ends and means can be achieved in the short run, and that the annual sequence automatically guarantees a dynamic efficiency in the use of resources.

Practical results are mixed. The mechanism has high informational requirements for central planners and large processing and coordination costs, yet no conduits have been set up to facilitate the supply of this type of information to planners. The absence of a functional price system implies that the economic actors themselves lack precise information about their own environment. Also, the vulnerability of the accounting system, monetary distortions, and the informal economy all suggest that the information reaching the central planners is insufficient and does not reflect the real conditions under which the economy operates. Unfortunately, the prevailing diagnosis attributes these defects to a lack of exigency and discipline in fulfilling the established procedures, rather than undertaking a deeper analysis of other countries' experiences or even that of Cuba. Even accepting that the long-run goals of these mechanisms are unchallengeable, empirical evidence casts great doubt on their viability.

Although this mechanism of central allocation is dominant in Cuba, there are some spaces for decentralized allocation of certain resources, even if their relative economic impact is small. These areas include the huge informal economy, nourished not only by resources diverted from the public sector but also by those from abroad. A noteworthy share of financing for many of the new private businesses evidently comes from relatives and friends living in other countries; it is well documented that significant quantities of consumer goods are individually imported, as are, increasingly, inputs and capital goods for their businesses.

New Sources of Accumulation

In smaller developing countries, given the insufficiency of domestic resources, access to foreign savings is generally key to assuring adequate levels of investment for economic and social development. Cuba is no exception. Since it lost the substantial foreign compensation from its ties with the CMEA, investment totals have been quite depressed. Although domestic resources are limited, a better use of domestic savings requires a financial system very different from the one that now exists. With the new credit policy adopted in 2011, opportunities to access loans in Cuban pesos from commercial banks expanded for certain purposes, including financing new private businesses. However, the drawn-out procedure and the size of the loans were not attractive to this sector. For non-state productive activity, the equivalent in $65.6 million dollars in credit was issued between 2011 and July 2015.

Considering current conditions, foreign savings will likely be key to increase current levels of accumulation significantly; altogether, they represent a potential contribution larger than what can be garnered from domestic sources. Because of a combination of adverse factors, over the past two decades Cuba has been regarded as a country of high financial risk. Among these factors are a poor credit history beginning with the 1986 unilateral suspension of payments to the Paris Club creditors, a situation finally normalized by the agreements of December 2015. Further, Cuba had not been a member of any multilateral financing body except for the International Investment Bank.[18] However, in September 2016 the Cuban Central Bank (Spanish initials BCC) signed an agreement with the Latin American Development Bank (Spanish initials CAF), which cemented the bases for future cooperation and a probable Cuban entrance as a CAF member.

Sovereign risk-assessment agencies incorporate these perceptions in their evaluation. Of the three best-known agencies, only Moody's began to assess the Cuban government financial position in 1999. Its initial rating of Caa1, lowered in April 2014 to Caa2, falls within the category of "junk debt," which means that any exposure to this debtor is considered high risk. Still, as a positive signal reflecting the thaw in relations with the United States, the continuity of the reforms, and reduced relative dependence on Venezuela, in December 2015 Moody's improved its prognosis from stable to positive, where it remained through the end of 2016 in spite of problems in external finances.

The steps mentioned in the previous sections are positive because they improve the nation's financial position, but Cuba must more actively use other channels, such as foreign investment. Although Cuba adopted a foreign investment law in 2005, the role of foreign direct investment has been much below the necessary level, and below the level that other countries have attracted over the same time (Pérez 2012).

The transformation program proposed a new view of the role of foreign investment. The initiative for the Mariel special development zone was launched in late 2013, and in March 2014 a new law was enacted (Law 118) to make the Zone more accessible for foreign investment. The Minister of Foreign Commerce and Investment has traveled to a number of countries to publicize the new regulations, and the role of coordinating further acts of promotion has been assigned to the Center for the Promotion of Foreign Commerce and Investment (ProCuba). Among the novelties are generous tax exemptions, changes in the role of the state employment agency as a hiring intermediary, and preparation of the so-called Portfolio of Investment Opportunities, which reflects the projects prioritized by the government. The impact of the new policy could grow if the rapprochement with the United States were to continue, given that this process has awakened great interest on the part of investors in that country and in other countries.

Nonetheless, although there has been an attempt to streamline the complex process of review and approval of proposals, the road toward adoption of the best international practices in this regard remains a long one. Three years after the Mariel project started, the approval of new projects was still very slow. Through June 2017, 24 projects had been approved, which is less than eight per year, This performance still does not match the priorities established for the country's development. Four of these projects involve exclusively Cuban capital.

Another source of current financing that has increased in importance since the 1990s is the flow of remittances. At the close of 2016, remittances represented a little more than 10% of total export value[19]—not a negligible amount, considering that this is a one-way flow and that the total does not include contributions in kind. Thus, there is a need for mechanisms to utilize remittances for productive ends and to multiply their impact on the economic fabric, something now happening informally in any case (Morales 2013). Taking into account the growing importance of these flows for developing countries, especially in Latin America, the authorities of several countries have developed initiatives to reorient a share of remittances toward productive sectors; these include programs to stimulate investments in buildings, savings accounts, and creating small and medium-sized businesses (Barceló 2013). The continuation of economic changes alongside the progressive elimination of restrictions limiting transactions between the United States and Cuba suggests that remittances could continue growing in the future. Therefore, it makes sense to design policies to maximize their economic impact within the Cuban economy.

What Model and How to Get There? The 2016 Seventh Party Congress Documents

The 2016 Seventh Congress of the Cuban Communist Party reaffirmed the continuity of the changes announced five years earlier. It recognized that only 22 percent of those guidelines had been completely fulfilled; these were issues that were easiest to resolve. The more difficult task began in 2016, with two elements of great import for the near future. First, Raúl Castro will turn the presidency over to a successor in February 2018, ending fifty-nine years of leadership marked by the roles of charisma and history in the exercise of politics. The new leader will face a very complex job of continuing the transformations. Second, in 2016 the economy entered another recessive cycle, once again occasioned primarily by difficulties facing Cuba's major trading partner, Venezuela. This confirms that not enough has been done since 2011.

The Seventh Congress approved two new documents to replace the first generation of Guidelines. The new documents are to guide the reforms of the coming year. They imply more extensive and elaborate changes, with a strategic horizon and, for the first time, they anticipate a time and place for arriving at the future.

The two main documents are conceived as a single body with conceptual consistency, while the revised version of the original Guidelines becomes a transitional document that establishes short-term benchmarks. The Conceptualization is the central theoretical and political document that describes the general outline of Cuba's future model. The 2030 National Development Plan tries to concretize that future in terms of social and economic policies, charting a path toward that desired end. This document presumes the release of a second part, not yet completed, that will set the quantitative goals to be achieved during the period. What follows analyzes and describes the merits and shortfalls of this overall proposal.

The Conceptualization states that the ultimate goal is the construction of socialism under Cuban conditions, a stipulation that establishes a distance from the experience of Eastern Europe and the former Soviet Union, and comes much closer to the processes in China and Vietnam. In light of the document's content and the probable means of implementation, one can more rigorously affirm that it is an attempt to sketch a specifically Cuban model that includes many elements shared by the rest of contemporary mixed economies.

Although the plan projects the supremacy of state property, it leaves ample room for other forms or property, sometimes in association with the state-owned sector. In addition, it legitimizes a shift toward more indirect means of state intervention in the economy. One section goes so far as to declare that "the state will concentrate on the functions appropriate to it, such as planning, regulating, conducting, and controlling the process of economic and social development . . . ," which is notably similar to the standards shared by modern states.

The document's diagnosis of the starting point goes beyond that put forward in the Guidelines, both in its language and in the weaknesses or problems to which it alludes. Among these are a lack of hard currency; technological backwardness; stunted productive base, infrastructure, and investment; and environmental damage. In addition, the overview of the situation recognizes a number of social difficulties such as growing inequality, domestic migration and foreign emigration of skilled labor, the existence of corruption, crime, and other forms of social marginality, and the demographic aging and stagnation of the population. Still, as could be expected, there are overestimations of the country's strengths. In this regard, two issues should have received more attention. Both relate to anchors of the Cuban model that are undergoing accelerated reconfiguration: the society's growing heterogeneity that stems originally from income differentiation but also has important ramifications in other areas, and the deterioration in the quality of social services, related to the topic of inequality.

One thing that stands out is the recognition that the Cuban model's sustainability depends directly on achieving greater development, which in turn is tightly linked to economic growth. One of the great mistakes of the Cuban process has been excessive reliance on voluntarism and political mobilization in the management of the economy. There is also clear recognition of existing dissatisfaction with delays in improving the economy. In this sense, the economy is the center and priority of the transformations under way. Linking the longevity of the model to progress, and not necessarily to the completion of the transition to socialism, marks a rupture with the previous discourse and probably opens the door to more pragmatic decisions that account for the rules of the game of today's world.

The primary form of property will be the socialist property of all the people, whose representatives will control the fundamental means of production in a context of coexistence with multiple other forms. This leads to interesting corollaries. The door opens to the possibility that these fundamental means could, on certain occasions, be shared or managed by the heads of other recognized forms. Moreover, the document declares that collective property entails both duties and rights, among which are direct participation in the administration of these goods, and further still, in making decisions about their use and management. Unfortunately, nothing is said about how this proposal is to be put into practice.

Similarly, the government envisions a broadening of the concept of mixed property, including the possibility that state enterprises could associate with other entities, both domestic and foreign. This would open a large spectrum of options that would tend to diversify further the types of property and management operating in the Cuban economy. A clear distinction is made between property and management, which points toward a significant increase in flexibility about forms of management that may include a variety of non-state forms.

One of the most expected and needed areas of change is the treatment of private property. The new multi-year strategy goes beyond all previous formulations. For the first time in the revolutionary period, it is clearly established that private property has a place and a social function in the Cuban model—it is subsidiary to the major forms, but still this is a great step forward, and if adequately implemented it could overcome various burdens that unnecessarily retard the development of productive forces.

The new strategy also clarifies that the regulations should allow all producers, regardless of their form of property, to have similar conditions for operation and similar access to markets. However, only with implementation will it become clear how the term "similar" will be interpreted, since it does not exactly mean "equal."

Alongside the changes in property structure, the documents bless a combination of direct and indirect instruments of state intervention in the economy; the proposals suggest that the indirect means will acquire new importance as the new model is rolled out. Rather than setting prices centrally with only a few exceptions, the state will establish price determination policies, transferring the actual setting of prices to the enterprise system.

As for social policy, it would have been desirable to recognize that notions of citizen prosperity are not limited just to domestic aspirations and circumstances, because these aspirations are increasingly influenced by consumption patterns and life styles coming from the largely capitalist outside world. This phenomenon is not exclusive to Cuba, but in Cuba it acquires particular characteristics. Cuba is Western, underdeveloped, and Latin American; it is near the United States and near the large Cuban community in that country and in others, with ever-strengthening ties to the nation of origin, a process favored by the reforms underway; and Cubans also have growing access to the Internet and mass media.

Further, the documents lay out a goal of guaranteeing economic and social stability, free of insecurities about family or personal futures. This is an excessively idealist project. The increase in uncertainty marks contemporary society, related to technical change and to the growing mobility and interaction of capital, jobs, and individuals. New opportunities appear while entire sectors are destroyed with a speed never before imagined.

The advance represented by the proposal is undeniable, but tensions and even contradictions persist that must be resolved for the program to be put into practice. Acceptance of a mixed economy faces a deliberate ranking of the different forms of property. The result is a scheme in which socialist property of all the people (state ownership) ranks as the main form, followed by cooperatives that receive special attention as a collective type of management, and finally private property as a subsidiary option. Yet the reach and the functions foreseen for private property suggest that foreign investment will play a leading role while domestic private capital will confront more limitations as to size and the sectors where it can exercise initiative.

The superiority of some forms over others is only an aspiration, one that answers to non-economic considerations; it is unachievable without profound changes in state enterprises. Overcoming capitalist relations is not something to be accomplished by decree. The proposed ranking can lead to inefficient allocation of productive factors, which will enormously retard the declared objective of economic growth, recognized as essential for the model's sustainability.

Likewise, if an administrative criterion prevails to determine which areas are open to the private sector and the rules of the market, then two counterproductive effects can be foreseen. One is that overall economic performance could be compromised if contradictions between the market and non-market sectors grow deeper. The evidence for this hypothesis is that, in only six years, the areas where private property operates have made both quantitative and qualitative leaps. The other effect is the generation of permanent stimulus for informality, which is in turn a breeding ground for tax evasion, corruption, and unchecked inequality.

Another controversial area is the role of the market, which continues to be regarded as an alternative to central planning. The latter is declared the main form of administration, without discussion of the coming deep changes in traditionally dominant concepts of planning. Officials even talk about deciding in which areas market relations will be accepted. This is an obvious contradiction because the market consists of objective social relations that do not depend on conscious recognition by any political or administrative entity. Additionally, process is wrongly conflated with tools, establishing a near-identity between planning and direct administrative tools. Empirical evidence shows that the best plan recognizes market disequilibria and uses direct actions in a circumstantial and transitory way because otherwise they permanently subvert fundamental economic signals.

The creation of limits on concentration of property and wealth is another far-reaching issue, given the interpretation of this principle since the adoption of the Guidelines in 2011. In general, it has imposed restrictions on the growth and development of the private sector. Besides impeding the use of clear standard rules for all actors, this constraint goes against the logic of economic progress. It is hard to understand how to establish economic growth as a central goal yet systematically penalize the most efficient and creative enterprises—those that grow and that acquire more productive factors, including a workforce. Not only does this compromise efficient allocation of resources but it also rewards poorer performance. By trying to level the best entities downward, it pushes the worst producers up.

Social appropriation of the larger share of riches, which should be the goal of the type of social justice that is possible in current conditions, can take place in a context in which state management and state property are not in the majority. It also requires that public entities be well managed and that there be social rewards for the best performers.

An encouraging sign is the recognition of the need for a more functional relationship with the world economy, as expressed in the declaration that economic integration with other countries will be promoted, especially within the Latin American region. However, advancing in this direction raises a substantive difficulty. In the contemporary world, global participation tends to involve deep integration of the participating economies. For some time, the negotiated agreements have gone beyond the realm of trade alone, to include investments, intellectual property, competition, and public procurement, among other areas. The existence of those areas assumes that the fundamental institutions of a market economy are operating in the participating economies. This is not the case in Cuba. Thus, the following dilemma arises: either those rules of the game are accepted on the assumption that long-run benefit is the key issue and the needed transformations are gradually introduced; or Cuba remains outside those processes, which in most cases extend beyond the bilateral arena.

The last word of the combined documents belongs to the 2030 National Development Plan. This is an ambitious proposal of great importance and reach, which also includes very significant methodological changes. One of these rejects the notion that development equals the evolution of economic sectors understood as branches of the economy. According to the Plan, these branches depend on a previous proposition that identifies so-called "strategic axes," understood as the transverse areas of transformation that will activate the levers needed to turn the nation's vision into a reality, an issue that transcends the purely economic sphere. It is an incomplete proposal, though, because indicators, gaps, and goals remain to be elaborated, as do the corresponding financing needs and possible sources.

Here another underlying ambiguity looms. Especially in view of the aspirations of both documents, substantial growth in productive investment is an indispensable condition for success. Yet the question of external financing gets only passing discussion, without explicit mention of international financial institutions. The outlined goals are not achievable, however, while the country remains alienated from these institutions, both those of a concessional nature (development banks like the World Bank or the Inter-American Development Bank) or those of a compensatory one (International Monetary Fund).

Closing Thoughts

The recent Communist Party Congress was the seventh since the triumph of the Revolution and the second of Raúl Castro's presidency. It generated great expectations and offered an ideal moment to assess what has been achieved. In many aspects, the Cuba of 2016 was very different from that of a decade earlier.

From 2007 to 2016, annual average growth in GDP was 2.4 percent, lower than the average for the whole period 1994–2016 or for the period 1994–2006. In any case, these figures are all modest and do not suggest improvement over the historical aggregate. A simple exercise in comparative statistics puts the number in context. At this rate, it would take Cuba nearly 27 years to reach Chile's 2015 per capita GDP, and eighty years to reach that of Singapore.[20] If judged against the aim to close the gap between Cuba and some other developing states, the current growth rate is indeed very modest. It is also below the goals set for the five-year period 2011–2015 and the projections of the 2030 National Development Plan. The economic slump of 2016 accentuates the need for a takeoff while rendering the possibility more distant.

There are some new elements in this era compared to earlier ones, which are worth underlining. First, the government launched the biggest reform of the Cuban economic model in the past fifty years, allowed a gradual but committed rapprochement with the United States, and modified the Constitution and the electoral laws. Second, it has been clearly understood that normalization of Cuba's international finances requires honoring signed commitments and accepting the basic rules governing world finance. This will be put to the test in the new international context; in July 2016, backlogs in payment to providers were accepted. At the same time, it might have been more advantageous to sign more accords with foreign businesses. In some cases, the debt renegotiations included creation of funds to support investment in Cuba. Such opportunities were greater after December 2014, when the process of Cuba-United States rapprochement was announced, turning world interest to Cuba.

Moreover, the approach to foreign capital suffers from other basic defects. A study carried out in 2012 clearly found that the existing tax system was a neutral element in assessments of Cuba as a potential place to invest. Still, the study identified other negative elements (labor regulations, legal framework, internal distribution channels, financial system, and authorization procedures) that had not been modified enough by new regulations. For example, the changes made in the system for hiring workers did not eliminate the state employment agency that retains a substantial portion of the wage or salary paid by the foreign employer. Likewise, a new form of intermediation between employers and employees is unwelcome by the majority of investors. In practice, this criticism would point toward a pattern of unbalanced incentives with a high fiscal cost without having the desired effect on potential investors. Evidently, there was not enough consensus to advance in a homogeneous way in all areas, which shows how controversial these issues are.

There has also been experimentation with a public debt market to finance up to 70 percent of the budget deficit, so far only through participation by state banks. This constitutes a necessary step toward relaxing the pressures on the state budget and making it possible to expand spending to stimulate demand. It also allows for de-linking the budget deficit from inflation, to the extent that it reduces the practice of printing money to finance the public sector. These two components could put authorities in a better position for a successful implementation of currency and exchange-rate unification. However, the long-term implications of this policy should be analyzed. First, it represents a loan from the rest of the economy to the public sector, principally based on household savings. The interest rate charged by the banks is set by the state, and it does not necessarily reflect the opportunity cost of those resources. Likewise, there is need for study of the effect on bank balance sheets.

In 2013 the administration announced the long-awaited transition toward a currency and exchange rate system more in tune with the needs of a modern economy. The opportunity to carry out transactions in either currency has been extended to most retail commerce, and instructions and preparations for the changeover to a new system are said to be forthcoming. However, even considering the risks and the necessarily gradual pace of these steps, the process has not moved at the speed anticipated by many, given the great expectations raised among individuals and economic actors. Prolonging this transition period has caused a clear re-conformation of the reserves and savings of the majority of those with substantial sums at play, requiring renewed dollarization of operations in certain areas, strengthening the informal hard currency market, and possibly sowing more doubts about the government's ability to carry the program through to a safe harbor.

It was announced in late 2014 that foreign exchange reserves had reached a total of $10 billion, providing a sizable cushion for the Central Bank, yet in some ways the current situation is more confusing than it was a few years ago. This confusion has happened because of the introduction of various partial exchange-rate schemes, such as those used by hotels to purchase agricultural products directly from producers. The balance-of-payment problems that appeared in 2016 and the return of dollarization suggest a more challenging context for moving ahead with unification plans that, at the same time, are indispensable to guarantee the success of still other changes.

This set of problems relates directly to the lack of correspondence between the changes in property structure and the mechanisms of resource allocation, which are designed to control all movements of factors and inputs in an economy where the state owns the majority of property. This disconnect has become more evident in recent years with the emergence of the self-employment activities and the cooperatives on the one hand, alongside the reinforcement of allocation mechanisms dependent on the government on the other. The central economic plan, the allocation of hard currencies, and foreign trade all operate under stricter limits today than they did in the 1990s. This generates two main problems. First, the non-state sector loses some of its significance because formal property ownership is not complete ownership from an economic point of view. If the owner of a business wants to increase production by purchasing more equipment, he or she will most likely resort to the informal market. This applies, for instance, to small farmers because there is no formal market in agricultural machinery such as tractors or irrigation equipment. The same can be said of capital. The backwardness of the Cuban financial system has stimulated informal financing, frequently from foreign sources, of a large share of new enterprises, which generates a number of challenges (Vidal 2013).

Additionally, there are signs of a separation between labor and other factors of production within the economy. The workforce is the most mobile of these factors, for a variety of reasons. In the previous model, its allocation could be oriented in accord with the preference of planners, with the supply dependent on the educational system directed by the authorities, and demand anticipated according to major investment plans. These plans often implied physical displacement within the nation's borders accompanied by the construction of new communities. Today, the public education system still largely determines the structure of abilities in the supply of the labor force, but other alternatives have begun to appear. In addition, the international mobility of the Cuban labor force has grown substantially in the past decade, especially since 2013 when new migration and travel rules were approved. Within the country, there are many more employment alternatives outside the state sector than there were a few years ago. In this new milieu the directed movement of the labor force toward other activities may not generate a proportional and parallel flow of capital and inputs; the result would be inefficient use of labor.

This rigidity translates to lower productivity and even de-skilling through at least two different scenarios. One assumes that these negative results are produced by regulations that impede creation of jobs demanding the same skill levels as the ones displaced, e.g., an engineer goes to work as a waiter or manager in a restaurant. If there is no opportunity to create a private specialized engineering services firm, the rejected post is replaced with one that offers higher income but wastes the skill abilities deposited in that worker. Even worse, the current restrictions keep that worker from becoming more productive over the long run. The reasons were discussed above: the enterprise cannot grow enough, cannot buy the necessary modern equipment, cannot expand its market beyond the country's borders, and has no access to a financial system or other sophisticated specialized services.

Important steps have been taken that begin to reveal the contours of a new economic model. However, its internal coherence is not guaranteed. Significant accomplishments have occurred in macroeconomic management, particularly in the external sphere and in fiscal policies and rules. Nonetheless challenges remain, associated with modifying the currency/exchange system and maintaining price stability in that context. There is a positive reorientation of investment toward material production and commercial services, and a more rapid increase in consumption relative to the rest of the components of aggregate demand. Still, that re-composition of the structure of accumulation is taking place in the midst of very depressed investment levels.

Substantial change can be seen in the property structure, not yet matched by resource allocation or by rules of the game necessary to improve the business climate. In the short run, this generates additional tension and threatens the improvement of efficiency and productivity. Inability to view and respond to these contradictions objectively could undermine the very strategic goals of change: economic efficiency and social equity.

Although it may seem improbable, the major challenges for the Cuban reform lie in the sphere of implementation. A series of elements is at play that goes beyond economic analysis. Among the obstacles confronting this critical phase are weak communication of goals to the public, interest groups that defend the middle administrative strata, lack of clarity in instructions from the highest levels of leadership, an absence of accountability with respect to publicly announced objectives, leakage of labor from the public sector, and ignorance about the minimum operating principles of a mixed economy, prominently including the rules of the game of the international economy and relations with foreign capital.

As a symptom of the political and ideological tensions that have an impact on the pace and scope of the reform, the granting of licenses in the most important categories within the private sector was temporarily suspended in the summer of 2017. In addition, the regulatory framework for the private and cooperative markets were being revised, a step that points toward more restrictive changes. Thus, the commitment to pragmatically implement the so-called "Conceptualization"—including measures already agreed upon—is up for discussion.

With these weaknesses and uncertainties, the path will remain twisted, and failure to meet milestones the rule rather than the exception. This was already seen in the 2011–2016 period. The new documents are sufficiently general to permit a wide spectrum of possible paths to implementation according to differing conceptions, correlations of forces, and economic needs. Worries about the impact on equity are legitimate. However, they should not excuse inaction. The panorama of the past twenty-five years displays the worst possible combination: weak economic growth alongside growing inequality. The very modest results achieved since the start of the reforms are an invitation to do more, better, and more rapidly—not less.

Notes

1. In the late 1980s, the housing stock deficit was calculated to be approximately 500,000 units (Rodríguez 1990).
2. The program of reforms first approved in April 2011 at the Sixth Congress of the Cuban Communist Party is officially titled the Guidelines of the Economic and Social Policy of the Party and the Revolution. A new version of this document emerged from the Seventh Party Congress in April 2016.
3. The theoretical-conceptual background for the Cuban model approved at the Seventh Congress of the Cuban Communist Party (April 2016) is officially called the Conceptualization of the Cuban Economic and Social Model of Socialist Development.
4. The document outlining the development program oriented toward the year 2030 in accordance with the previous economic reform documents. Its full title is the National Plan for Economic and Social Development through 2030: A Vision of the Nation and Its Strategic Axes and Sectors. The Conceptualization details the "what"; the Development Plan 2030 can be described as the "how."
5. The method of calculating GDP changed since 2003, essentially awarding greater weight to social services. The growth in foreign sales of such services implied growth in this main component of GDP, which favored high statistical growth rates.
6. This includes purchases of food from the United States, which in the 2010s became much less attractive because of the severe payment conditions they carry.
7. The debt to that country was recognized by Cuba only to the extent that its negotiation would include compensation for the damage suffered from abrupt cancellation of contracts signed with the Soviet Union. Also, Cuba objected to the method used to calculate the total, given that the debts had originally been in convertible rubles, a currency that no longer existed, and Russia had applied an arbitrary exchange rate to denominate them in U.S. dollars.
8. The Paris Club is an informal group made up of the main state-bank creditors whose mission is to find coordinated, sustainable solutions for debtor

countries having difficulties making payments. Since its founding in 1956, it has been the framework for signing 433 accords with 90 countries around the world.

9. The London Club is an informal group of private creditors, constituted to coordinate negotiations with countries facing difficulties in their debt payments. It parallels the Paris Club, which is made up of public-sector creditors.

10. On 8 April 2015, Reuters reported this figure after an exchange of emails with Nicholas Berry, president of Stancroft Trust, one of the largest private holders of Cuban debt. The report said that a committee had been created within the Club to analyze the Cuban debt issue.

11. Chapter IV, Investment Policy, Guideline number 118.

12. Díaz-Briquets (2015) analyzed population projections from several institutions in Cuba and from the United Nations. The data indicated that the working-age population would begin to contract around the year 2015, and relations of dependency would increase, both tendencies accelerating in later periods.

13. At the end of 2014, real wages were equivalent to 35 percent of the 1988 level (author's calculation). However, in 1989 wages were the principal (and often the only) source of income for the immense majority of families, which was not the case by 2016. Thus wages are not a trustworthy indicator of Cuban purchasing power.

14. In April 2016, for a selected group of products, the Cuban government reduced CUC retail prices by 20 percent. Some of these are basic food items. Still, problems of availability recurred throughout 2016.

15. Law 117 on foreign investment, approved in March 2014 by the National Assembly in a special session, includes all sectors except education, public health, and defense as potential areas for foreign investors. However, domestic private investment is restricted to a small list of activities, mostly in simple services and light manufacturing. Theoretically, cooperatives may participate in all spheres; in practice, through 2015 the sectoral profile of cooperatives has been very similar to that of "self-employment." That issue is addressed more directly in other chapters within this book.

16. An important difference, besides the long-term goals of the transformation, has to do with the role assigned to cooperatives, as a form of property that is more collective than purely private business but useful, in principle, for dealing with many of the weaknesses of traditional state enterprises.

17. This dual system is, in the last analysis, a response to a fundamental problem: the chronic scarcity of hard currencies, which in turn stems from a deficit in the balance of payments. The system permits, temporarily, the centralized allocation of hard currency in accord with the "systemic" importance of the use—i.e., imports of food, energy, basic products, etc. Such arrangements have been tried out in other contexts in the past; in 2014, two other Latin American countries, Argentina and Venezuela, also employed multiple exchange rates as well as exchange controls. In general, these methods are very costly

and inefficient; they should be retired as soon as possible. The difficulty in the Cuban case lies in the length of time the scheme has been in place and as part of larger set of centralized mechanisms for allocating resources. Therefore, the economy has been subject to profound distortions during a prolonged period, with very deleterious effects statistically and dynamically (in terms of behavior, preferences, and the informal economy).

18. The International Investment Bank is a multilateral development bank established in 1970 within the Council for Mutual Economic Aid (CMEA). The institution continued operating after demise of CMEA, and in this century it has been revitalized with Russian support. It is a small bank, with nine current members including Cuba.

19. This calculation is based on a total of about $1.5 billion in annual remittances, drawn from a review of several sources making such estimates, which vary considerably according to the methodology employed. Though the estimate may appear low, it shows that remittances are a significant source, to which may be added the remittances in kind.

20. The numbers for GDP per capita for Chile and Singapore are taken from the World Development Indicators in constant 2010 dollars. For Cuba, GDP per capita comes from the *Anuario Estadístico de Cuba 2016*; it assumes that Cuban pesos (CUP) are equivalent to current dollars.

Bibliography

Barceló, Anabel. 2013. "Institucionalización del mercado de remesas en América Latina y el Caribe: un decenio de transformaciones." In *Revista del Banco Central de Cuba*, 16: 4.

Castro, Raul. 2009. "Intervención ante el período de sesiones de la Asamblea Nacional del Poder Popular." December, Havana.

Díaz-Briquets, Sergio. 2015. "Major Problems, Few Solutions: Cuba's Demographic Outlook." In *Cuban Studies* 43:3–18.

Espina, Mayra. 2012. "La política social en Cuba: nueva reforma económica." In *Revista de Ciencias Sociales de Costa Rica* 135–136:227–236.

Ferriol, Angela. 2004. "Política social y desarrollo: una aproximación global." In Jorge Mattar and Elena Alvarez, *Política social y reformas estructurales: Cuba a principios del siglo XXI*. Mexico City: CEPAL.

Figueras, Miguel Alejandro. 1999. *Aspectos estructurales de la economía cubana*. Havana: Editorial Ciencias Sociales.

García, Anicia, Susanne Gratius, and Luisa Íñiguez. 2013. "Entre universalidad y focalización: los desafíos sociales en Cuba en el contexto latinoamericano." In José A. Alonso and Pavel Vidal, *¿Quo Vadis, Cuba? La incierta senda de las reformas*. Madrid: Catarat, 189–225.

González, Ivet. 2011. "The Sharp Edge of Change." Inter Press Service, February 11.

Hidalgo, Vilma, and Anabel Barceló. 2012. "Cuasifiscalidad: un punto en la agenda sobre fiscalidad en Cuba." In *Cofin Habana* 2.

León, Jessica, and David Jesús Pajón. 2015. "Política crediticia en Cuba: evolución reciente y efectos sobre el sector no estatal." In Omar Everleny Pérez and Ricardo Torres, *Miradas a la Economía Cubana. Análisis del sector no estatal.* Havana: Editorial Caminos, 103–144.

Mesa, Natacha Teresa. 2015. "Cooperativas no agropecuarias: razones para un nuevo cuerpo legal cooperativo en Cuba." In Omar Everleny Pérez and Ricardo Torres, *Miradas a la Economía Cubana. Análisis del sector no estatal.* Havana: Editorial Caminos, 63–74.

Mesa-Lago, Carmelo, and Pavel Vidal. 2009. "The Impact of the Global Crisis on Cuba's Economy and Social Welfare." In *Journal of Latin American Studies* 42:689–717.

Morales, María Isabel. 2013. *Revista del Banco Central de Cuba.* Consulted 12 April 2014 at http://www.bc.gob.cu/anteriores/RevistaBCC/2013/Rev%201%20 WEB%202013/Balance%20del%20SBN.html.

ONEI. Various years. *Anuario estadístico de Cuba.* Havana: Oficina Nacional de Estadística e Información.

Pérez, Omar Everleny. 2012. "Foreign Direct Investment in China, Vietnam and Cuba: Pertinent Experiences for Cuba." In Jorge Domínguez, Omar Everleny Pérez, Mayra Espina and Lorena Barbería, *Cuban Economic and Social Development. Policy Reforms and Challenges in the 21st Century.* Cambridge: Harvard University Press, 193–226.

Piñero, Camila. "Nuevas cooperativas cubanas: logros y dificultades." In Omar Everleny Pérez and Ricardo Torres, *Miradas a la Economía Cubana. Análisis del sector no estatal.* Havana: Editorial Caminos, 51–62.

Rodríguez, José Luis. 1990. *La estrategia de desarrollo económico de Cuba.* Havana: Editorial Ciencias Sociales.

Roselló, Diana. 2013. "Mercado Interbancario en Cuba." Doctoral thesis, Universidad de La Habana.

Torres, Ricardo. 2014. "Transformations in the Cuban Economic Model. Context, General Proposal, and Challenges." In *Latin American Perspectives*, 41:4, 74–90.

UNCTAD. *UNCTADStat.* 25 de agosto de 2017. http://unctadstat.unctad.org/wds/ReportFolders/reportFolders.aspx (acceso: 20 de agosto de 2014).

Vidal, Pavel. 2013. "La apertura a las microfinanzas en Cuba." In Omar Everleny Pérez and Ricardo Torres, *Economía cubana: ensayos para una reestructuración necesaria.* Havana: Instituto de Información Científica y Tecnológica, 46–69.

3

The Planning Paradigm in Cuba: Tethering the Economic Takeoff

Oscar Fernández Estrada

The First Decades

The first systematic efforts at planning on a country-wide scale emerged in Cuba after the triumph of the Revolution of 1959. To be sure, in 1952 the Junta Nacional de Economía was created as a consultative body to coordinate state economic planning and government programs and, in 1955, the Junta Nacional de Planificación emerged, also as a consultative body advising the executive branch. However, these institutions generally dealt with formalities or efforts with minor effects. In 1960, these two bodies were replaced by the Junta Central de Planificación,[1] a collaborative entity at the ministerial level, led at that time by Prime Minister Fidel Castro, that included the Ministers of Commerce, Banking, Treasury, Public Works, Labor, Agrarian Reform, and Economics.[2]

At that time, the concepts and methods of planning of most common international use were introduced in Cuba, brought mainly from countries of a socialist orientation, with participation by important foreign economists linked to that system.[3] However, the reach of these methods was limited by the inherited structure of property, which contained only an incipient presence of nationalized means of production. With the radicalization of the revolutionary process, that presence soon grew larger, to be felt in all spheres of the economy and society.[4]

The 1960s and early 1970s brought experimentation—largely unproductive—with a variety of centralized management mechanisms for the new planned economy. This was followed by a period of planning coordinated with the USSR, as part of which Cuba joined the Council for Mutual Economic Aid (CMEA)[5] in 1972. This context created the basis for approval, at the First Congress of the Cuban Communist Party in 1975, of the Sistema de Dirección y Planificación de la Economía, a mechanism largely similar to the economic model prevailing in the Soviet Union.[6] The administration developed a system of planning based fundamentally on centralized material balance sheets[7] linked to commitments for foreign trade within the CMEA. Cuba's international trade was thus being carried out and accounted for in physical terms, while financial categories were less important; this approach generated distortions in the measurement of costs, efficiency, and productivity. Extremely vertical supply plans, based on one-year and five-year projections of what would be received from the CMEA, tended to inhibit development of horizontal linkages among enterprises, because their inputs were assigned from above and their products generally had predetermined destinations. In sum, the planning mechanism almost completely replaced the market[8] as the coordinator of interactions among agents, under the assumption that this was the nature of a socialist economy.

Table 3.1: National Plans since the Triumph of the Revolution

- Development Plan for 1962.
- Medium-term (four-year) plan, 1962–1965.
- From that date on, Annual Plans have been created.
- Projections 1962–1965.
- Projections 1966–1970.
- Projections 1971–1975.
- Projections 1971–1980.
- Five Year Plan 1976–1980 (beginning along with International Coordination of Plans).
- Five Year Plan 1981–1985.
- Five Year Plan 1986–1990.
- Economic and Social Development Plan through 2000 (developed from 1978 on, and submitted for government consideration in mid-1984).
- Economic Development Scenarios 1997–2000.
- Economic Development Scenarios 2001–2005.
- Special and Branch Plans.
- Projection 2010–2015.
- Economic and Social Development Plan for 2030 (in process of elaboration).

Source: Constructed by the author on the basis of JUCEPLAN (1985).

Although mercantile relations expanded slightly at the end of the 1970s, and private, mostly agricultural markets appeared, the state did not design economic mechanisms to regulate them, trying instead, fruitlessly, do so through administrative and political methods. The consequences of that effort were deemed harmful to Cuban socialism, and so this policy was reversed as part of the process called "Rectification of Errors" initiated at the Third Congress of the Cuban Communist Party (CCP) in the mid-1980s. Thus, from 1959 until the collapse of the Soviet

Union at the beginning of the 1990s, Cuba did not develop any financial mechanisms of importance.

The New Mechanism of the 1990s
In the early 1990s, with the crumbling of the socialist bloc and end of its trade arrangements, Cuba's channels of foreign trade disappeared almost completely. The country sank into a severe crisis. Gross domestic product (GDP) dropped approximately thirty-five percent, a circumstance further aggravated by the U.S. government's decision to tighten its commercial and financial blockade.[9] Consequently the mechanism of planning through material balances was orphaned by the lack of trade ties. Between 1992 and 1994, for instance, no National Economic Plan was issued. The budget was reestablished only in 1994 through Decree-Law 148, and the plan was once again approved by the National Assembly of People's Power in 1995.

Eventually a different model arose. It was a type of financial planning new in the Cuban context—although, of course, a subset of fundamental physical balance sheets remained in use, including those for food, fuel, and some construction materials. The new model gave state enterprises broad powers—including that of carrying out foreign trade—in order to produce a quick reinsertion into the world economy.

The tactic of dividing the economy into two sectors, so as to try to cordon off the enormous monetary and financial distortions in one of them identified as the traditional sector, while smoothing the path of the so-called emerging sector (free of initial disequilibria), involved acceptance of a process of partial dollarization that would become a crucial tool of economic recovery.

The increased decentralization of this period did not mean a decrease in the state's role in centralized resource allocation, but rather the appropriate selection of more efficient mechanisms. The so-called Hard Currency Revenue and Spending Budget was the basic tool for managing the economy. Through this instrument, the state acted as provider of working capital or investor, while enterprises had the responsibility of recovering the investment and providing income to the state in accordance with a production plan; the enterprise was given autonomy to incur some expenditure on its own behalf.

The guiding document of state policy approved in 1997, the Economic Resolution of the Fifth Congress of the CCP, described what had been implemented during that period: "Planning is shifting from an excessively centralized model based on material balance sheets to another one—still in process of implementation—that will promote valuation and financial balances of external resources and other definitions and means of coordination, integrating all forms of property under the predominance of state property" (PCC, 1997). This transformation was key to reversing the deep economic depression that the country confronted during the 1990s. Nonetheless, paradoxically, it did not serve as a point of departure for a true reconstruction of the theoretical paradigm of planning. Rather, a few years later the extremes of centralization returned.

In the middle of the 2000–2009 decade, in the midst of a campaign to recover and develop the quality of social services diminished by the crisis, and with the country affected by severe natural disasters and facing a possible shock to the electrical generating capacity, among other issues, the state turned back to the use of more centralized mechanisms, especially for allocation of convertible currencies.[10] These were truly difficult and complex years, yet they coincided with a degree of economic bonanza for Cuba's trade balance because professional services provided by Cubans in Venezuela were paid for through petroleum imports—an exchange highly favorable to Cuba's economy.

Also in this period, many social programs sought to improve living conditions of Cubans. Many had a positive impact for the majority of the population. Others encountered disorder and improvisation in their implementations, even giving rise to episodes of corruption. Some, although worthy in their aims, were simply unsustainable given the economic conditions of an underdeveloped country, and ended up supported by resources taken from productive activities that were key for longer-term development.

Those and several other factors surely influenced the authorities' decision to reverse the process of decentralization that had supported recovery. However, the larger reason for the reversal, just as in the 1970s, lies in the incompatibility of a decentralized economic management system with a political system granting absolute power to the central levels. At some point this inconsistency becomes unsustainable and the solution ends up favoring economic centralization, which is the more conservative option.

The Context of "Updating"

Although the economy experienced a certain amount of recovery after the collapse, it still had not found a sustainable path. Growth rates slowed to between 1% and 3% a year, insufficient to overcome structural deformations and focus on problems of development. The persistence of powerful disequilibria and distortions in the macroeconomic sphere, which even threatened the short- and medium-term sustainability of the "social conquests" of the Revolution, was probably the main motivation leading the Sixth Congress of the CCP in 2011 to make transformation of the economic model its central concern.

Some external phenomena had negative impacts during this more recent period. For instance, according to official reports (PCC 2011), between 1997 and 2009 price fluctuations for exports and imports produced a net loss for the country of $10.9 billion in relation to 1997 levels. On average, the buying power of goods exports dropped by fifteen percent. Also the blockade (embargo) established by the United States adopted more rigorous mechanisms for penalizing Cuba's international economic activities. During this period numerous fines were imposed on foreign banks for accepting financial transactions to or from the island.[11] To complicate the situation further, severe weather caused great damage to the economy.[12]

However, some compensating elements also emerged. Such was the case of the decision of Venezuela's then-president Hugo Chavez to treat Cuban exports of professional services to Venezuela (carried out as part of social programs of support and solidarity) as tradable goods. Another influence was the 2004 emergence of the Bolivarian Alliance for the People of Our America (Spanish initials ALBA), which strengthened Cuban sources of income from delivery of such services in other countries of the region.[13]

In the domestic sphere, some substantive problems were diagnosed by the same Party Congress (PCC 2011):

- Existence of idle land and low agricultural yields;
- Diminished export capacity in traditional export lines;
- Low level of diversification in goods and services exports;
- High import dependence leading to strong financial constraints;
- Continued process of decapitalization of industry and productive infrastructure;
- Constraints on enterprises' and regions' ability to make their economic development more sustainable;
- Over-staffing in the state sector of the economy (inflated payrolls) generating workforce under-utilization, low productivity, and low wages;
- Excessively egalitarian mechanisms of income distribution provide equal treatment to unequal subjects and generate weak and distorted incentive systems;
- Weaknesses in the levels of coordination of macroeconomic policies and deep distortions deriving from the dual currency and exchange system;
- The prevailing planning system becomes unable to correct structural disproportions.

Among the most important implicit goals of the reform process undertaken in this period were more flexibility in relations among economic actors and recognition of new forms of non-state property, including small private businesses; and the redesign of management models of state enterprises in an attempt to give them greater autonomy in pursuit of increased effectiveness.

A third objective, perhaps more important for purposes of this study, is a methodological transformation in planning that stems from a recognition of the objective existence of the market in the economy.[14] However, the declaration of this objective was limited to establishing principles and did not suggest how such a transformation would be carried out.

Five years later, at the Seventh Party Congress in April 2016, the persistence of this recognition remained evident. The first guideline of the main Congress document says: "Socialist planning will still be the main means of directing the economy and will continue its transformation, guaranteeing fundamental macroeconomic equilibria and the objectives and goals of Social and Economic Development over the long term. Recognizing the objective existence of market relationships, [planning] influences the market and takes its characteristics into account" (PCC 2016a). Although five years had passed since this goal was set, so far there has not been sufficient progress in defining what aspects should change so as to successfully confront the new conditions and at the same time guarantee the leading role of a specific form of planning.

Meanwhile, the form in which productive processes have been regulated on a national scale in recent years has inhibited the full deployment of productive forces, though it does constitute an effort to manage the pressures of constant disequilibria generated by latent structural weaknesses. Instead, planning should play a leading role in economic growth and development.

The Idea of Planning: Etymological Traps

In the history of all attempts at socialist construction that have followed the Soviet model, state intervention has regularly taken a highly centralized and detailed form. The directive nature attributed to so-called socialist planning, which has been accepted as the fundamental hallmark distinguishing socialist planning from any attempts at planning or programming of capitalist economies, has enshrined the intent to manage directly a broad and complex range of details of a nation's economic life from a single center. The assumed logic implies an attempt to predetermine *a priori* most of the relations established among economic actors. That is, it assumes that practically no allocative solution can take place through the market.[15]

That approach offers the possibility of undertaking large adjustments in the national economy without exposure to inertial processes, but it also generates very high transaction costs given that central planners are unable to offer optimal solutions in a systematic manner. The incapacity to process rigorously each of the many elements to be centrally decided leads to a predominance of discretional behaviors at higher levels; on many occasions these decision makers underestimate or fail to recognize avoidable negative consequences deriving from completely foreseeable reactions by economic agents.

That inability to forecast generates a multiplicity of distorted behaviors among managers. In the first place, during the process of negotiating plans, enterprises tend to request more inputs than they really need and report less capacity than they really have, because they are conscious that the higher officials always will demand more than the enterprises can achieve and will assign them fewer inputs than they request. Hence the rational behavior is to hoard inventories to guarantee the continuity of production in case of some problems with supply or delayed authorizations. On many occasions, chain reactions of nonpayment among enterprises can easily arise, owing to a central constraint or delayed allocation of an input, which in turn affects the output of a given product line, with linked impacts on other lines.[16]

In sum, the notion of planning that predominates in Cuba comes from two major sources: one, the theoretical paradigm that emanated from Soviet practice and scholarship; and two, the result of institutional arrangements that have grown up since the 1990s to administer the economy. These are synthesized in Table 3.2.

Thus, Cuba's officials and academics and the general public all find themselves trapped in a definition of planning that is dysfunctional and obsolete for the direction that the government itself is trying to generate through the reform now under way.[17]

Centralized Mediation to Address Dual Currency Distortions

An element with significant influence on this etymological trap is associated with the dual currency system, and especially with the coexistence of two very different exchange rates for sectors of economic activity that are, necessarily, connected.[18]

In 1994, in a strategic measure undertaken to emerge from the crisis, the administration created a system of partial dollarization, with two monetary circuits running parallel to each other: one using the traditional Cuban peso (CUP) and the other using the U.S. dollar. Obviously, this also created two spaces in which each segment of the economy (individuals and enterprises) could access the supply of goods and services available in each currency. Thus there are agents with access to pesos and agents with access to dollars who, on many occasions, require exchange operations to fill their baskets of goods and services. They link through exchange markets.

Table 3.2: Factors That Nourish the Prevailing Cuban Planning Paradigm	
"Socialist" planning paradigm: *mechanism for allocating resources, fully replacing the market*	Money plays a generally passive role in the economy.
	Emphasis on use value, with focus on the concept of *needs* but minimizing the notion of *demand*.
	Constraints in the economy are generally manifested in physical terms, given that resource allocation takes place basically in such terms.
	The financial constraints on enterprises are weak. Vertical directives that assign tasks and resources are what constrain enterprises.
	Regulating processes through direct mechanisms requires a near-absolute predominance of state property.
Circumstances and institutional arrangements adopted in Cuba after the crisis of the 1990s	As a result of constant partial adjustments, an excessively fragmented price-setting system arose, lacking mechanisms for updating, and given its incoherencies made it unprepared to reflect real equivalencies.
	A tendency to generate specific regulatory frameworks, inhibit integrated solutions, and favor discretionality more than clear rules strengthens the need for verticalism.
	Persistent, complex dual-currency environment provokes isolation or disconnection among internal and external financial flows.
	Management of this disconnect—especially since 2008—occurs through systematic intervention from central levels that attempt to mediate and decide on every proposed transaction.
	Immense demands on the operational sphere, which end up diverting attention from long-range perspectives.

Source: Constructed by the author.

Individuals have a market to buy and sell dollars at an exchange rate of 1 USD = 25 CUP.[19] Enterprises (legal persons) receive centralized allocation of hard currencies to be bought with their pesos at an officially established rate of 1:1. This dual exchange system requires central authorities to mediate on almost all decisions that imply the use of hard currency.

Until 2003, enterprises with some hard currency income had a degree of autonomy in the use of this revenue in the context of these hard currency revenue and expenditure budgets. In 2004, when the dollar completely disappeared from internal circulation,[20] the authorities did not eliminate the duality but rather replaced the dollar with a Convertible Cuban peso

(CUC) at an exchange rate of approximately 1:1, maintaining the previous two circuits and their general characteristics. In other words, enterprises that had bought and sold in dollars now denominated their accounts in CUCs; when they needed to make a purchase abroad, they first converted CUCs into dollars. If there had been strict adherence to the rules about the replacement of USD by CUC, in theory they would have been guaranteed full convertibility between the two at an exchange rate of 1:1.

However, the de-dollarization of the economy greatly complicated a monetary policy that involved the domestic issuance of two currencies. As the report to the Party Congress showed, the economy faced limitations in confronting balance-of-payments deficits, high totals of debts became due, and banks began withholding international transfers (PCC 2011).

This complexity brought forth a new intervention tool—the so-called Certificate or Coefficient of Liquidity (CL), which granted CUC convertibility to enterprises that needed hard currency to make payments to foreign entities. To meet enterprises' demand for dollars, the central authorities must plan and engage in intense operational negotiations that take into account the activities to be carried out with this hard currency, the product lines to be imported, the commitments that must be honored, and the social goals to be fulfilled. The result is a perennial struggle involving incalculable trade-offs.

Figure 3.1: Mediating Mechanisms in Cuban Monetary Circuits

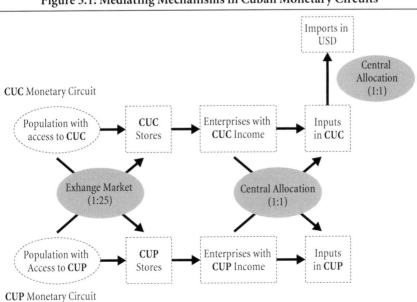

In conclusion, because the balance of payments constitutes the most critical variable, the monetary circuits are highly fragmented, and the price systems suffer from a high level of disconnection,[21] authorities have few operational options for centrally controlling external distributions. Thus the mechanism allocates resources within the economy in vertical fashion and largely in physical terms, and it maintains central controls over the prices of intermediate and final goods. This circumstance leads to the formulation of directives at all levels to regulate and restrict the physical consumption of a great number of product lines. This is true even for enterprises that, in theory, have the financial resources to acquire those goods in one of the local currencies. For instance, enterprises may get insufficient allocations of fuel or confront constraints on electricity consumption,[22] as well as face limitations on increasing production that involves imported components.

Figure 3.2: Circular Flow of Income in Cuba

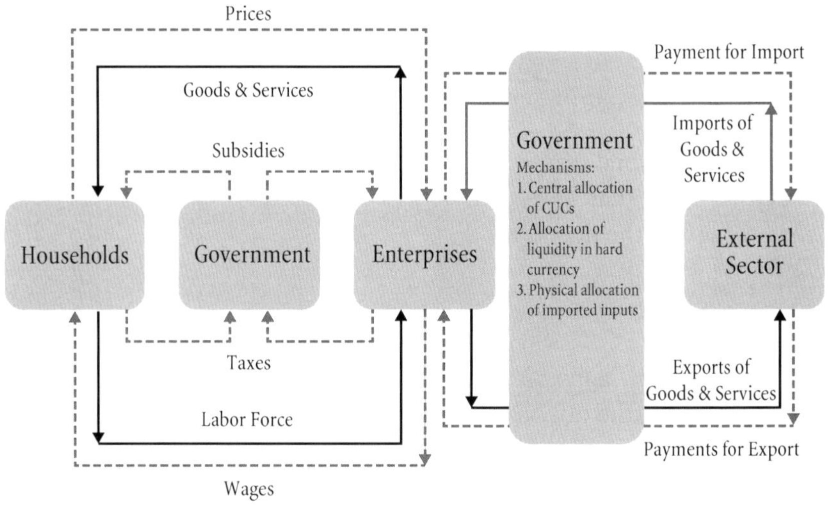

In sum, the absence of a single exchange rate to guarantee convertibility requires, in practice, the use of systematic mediation.[23] Attempts to correctly assign hard currency have led to the imposition of material regulation on production processes, which multiplies the spiral of other mediations, increases the probability of erroneous allocations, and further encourages the path of discretionality.

Three years ago, when the authorities announced the beginning of a process of currency reunification, new experimental exchange rate schemes were created for some actors in agriculture, tourism, and foreign investment; these regimes employed rates that were devalued with respect to the official one (1:1) and overvalued with respect to that of the population sector (1: 25). Since then, the process of reunification seems to have come to an inconclusive halt, but the multiplicity of exchange rates has remained in force, still complicating the mediations and allocation of resources.

The Necessary Transformation

Although the Ministry of Economics and Planning has sometimes seemed the entity most interested in decentralizing power to the enterprises, it is trapped in its own administrative mechanism. In general, the interpretation of *planning* enshrined in Cuba is an operational mechanism of systematic administrative mediation in search of a fairer allocation of resources within unfavorable circumstances, allegedly capable of replacing the market's role as coordinator of interactions among agents.

This situation has serious implications for guiding the Cuban economy. First, it requires a very costly process of coordination. The forecasts that are typically produced and reproduced inhibit the emergence of almost all initiative at the enterprise level; the congenital rigidity is an obstacle to rapid adaptation to changing conditions and results in allocations that are far from optimal or opportune. Further, the constant attempt to deal with bottlenecks that strangle the economy becomes the center of attention, preventing the development of a more global, long-term vision. The problem cannot be solved within this paradigm.

The 2016 Seventh Party Congress showed the intention to focus on a more distant horizon, but the National Economic and Social Development Plan (PCC 2016b) approved at the Congress will need to confront some weaknesses from the outset. The country's almost total lack of experience in this sort of exercise is well known (and somewhat paradoxical). The last time a study with such a distant time horizon was attempted was in the 1980s, when a development plan extending to the year 2000 was created. The several decades spent administering constant crises practically eliminated long-term thinking from the organizational culture. Sadly, Cuba also lacks institutes, centers, or state agencies to design, analyze, and examine possible futures, and it faces a relative scarcity of experts even in its academic sector.

Risks also arise in the process of shaping extended plans. The PCC's long-term plan contains clear references to a notion of development that extends beyond the economic sphere. The strategic axes identified in this plan involve government effectiveness, social integration, natural resources and environment, human development, equity and social justice, international insertion, infrastructure, science-technology-innovation, and more.[24] Nonetheless, the prevailing and deeply rooted vision of planning threatens to skew this plan in practice toward the transformation of the productive structure. This would not be a major evil if it finally were to remedy coherently the severe structural deformities that have held back the economy for decades. But, given the lack of input-output information, a failure to recognize sectoral interdependencies can lead to bottlenecks or to mismatches among conflicting goals. That is one of the greatest obstacles to constructing such a Development Plan: lack of quality information about inter-sectoral relations, and more important still, the potential distortion of any measurement of value in the economy given the dual currency system with its multiple exchange rates. Without resolving these issues, it will be very difficult to build a coherent long-run plan that would not turn out to be a disconnected checklist of objectives with unknown interdependencies.

Even after the implementation of the first groups of measures proposed in the reform process, the meager growth rates of past six years[25] show the need to inject new life into administrative mechanisms and management of the economy. Among the basic elements essential to transforming the concept of planning that now stifles the Cuban economy, a primary need is to embrace development as a system of goals and the long run as the determining horizon. At the same time, the now-undeniable non-state forms, which are emerging with agility in Cuba's midst, should be definitively accepted and considered in the design of objectives and policies, and therefore in the process of planning. Thus the use of guided markets should be expanded to serve as a mechanism to allocate resources throughout the economy.

This does not mean abandoning the centrality of planning and surrendering to the anarchic rationality of the disparate agents. But it does imply a profound change of concept based on the development of indirect regulatory mechanisms. This change requires introducing a framework within which financial regulation becomes the norm. The most evident superiority of such a framework rests in its ability to reduce complexity and rigidity in the process of resource allocation. Under this logic, there would be a gradual transition to market-driven resource allocation throughout the economy , monitored by the state and regulated as becomes necessary.

At the same time, the state should not give up its legal capacity to be the central allocator of physical resources in exceptional situations, given the advantages this offers in terms of a high degree of selectivity, immediacy, and maneuverability when it is directed only toward key aspects.

Another important issue is supplies in Cuban markets. In general, each product line's production is concentrated in one or a few enterprises. This could be justified in terms of the pursuit of supposed economies of scale derived from specialization; however, the main benefit is the ease it offers to centralized systems in confronting producers and even in interfering in their management, because there are so few of them.

In the future, in order for the elements of the system to function coherently under new conditions, production needs to be organized in such a way as to avoid artificial concentration[26] of high market shares in one or a few producers, whether state-owned or not.[27] It is particularly absurd and ineffective for such market shares to be awarded to foreign partners so they may enjoy easy conditions without the stress of competition within the Cuban economy.[28]

A great part of the effort should focus on ensuring that, in the markets for goods and services, the majority of the products should be determined by demand and not by supply, so as to overcome the current situation known as the "tyranny of the producers" (Brus 1969).

Final Considerations

After almost six decades of centralized administration of the Cuban economy, which has commonly been referred to as planning, a long list of impacts can be attributed to it. Without attempting to offer such an ambitious inventory, at least two very important legacies should be underlined. On the one hand, the process has been a guarantor of a set of social advances, preserving them from the impacts of successive economic crises. On the other, centralized planning may have thoroughly inhibited the development of an efficient state enterprise system, given the excess of regulations affecting those enterprises and the constant interference in their management.

The call for "Updating" the model, through a powerful official push augmented by popular participation, evidenced a vigorous consensus about the need for change. Nonetheless, the real possibilities of implementing transformations depend on a complex of factors that seem to outweigh the political leadership's will for change. There is a clash between the memory of nearly sixty years of an almost static centralized model and the manifest intent to modify it substantially. The result is a complex dynamic of construction-destruction of concepts, which will require years of coexistence and, simultaneously, inconsistencies and natural conflicts.

At the beginning of the reform process launched by President Raúl Castro, strong signals were sent about future institutional changes to make economic mechanisms more flexible and efficient. However, in the process of shaping the required new institutions, at least three contending cultural perspectives are at work.

First, there is the system of formal behavioral norms and prevailing legal regulations, now in process of modification toward the declared goal of advancing toward more plural, less discretional, and more economically rational forms of management.

Second, in clear confrontation with the first, there is the underlying entrenched political way of getting things done by a "know-how" well-rooted in officialdom at all levels. The habitual practices shaped during decades of vertical management have acquired cultural staying power, creating tacit norms that operate even outside what is explicitly regulated. The administrative heritage includes a constant prevalence of discretionality over rules, which constitutes one of the main barriers to self-transformation of the model.

The third dimension is the most vital, the one that in the final analysis sanctions socially accepted values and converts them into authentic laws that shape the true course of the society, what we might call the "social regulatory framework." This is unavoidably determined by the objective conditions facing the country. The educational system and political guidance can exercise determinant influences, but they can never supplant the role of the real forces of daily experience in establishing social standards of behavior.

The evolution of Cuban society in the future will depend on the vector of forces resulting from the permanent confrontation among these three dimensions.

It is praiseworthy that the process of transformation given official approval in 2011 mobilized cohesive support for the essential ideas of change, but no mechanisms have yet been designed to institutionalize social scrutiny of implementing the corresponding policy decisions . The long history of the Revolution offers varied examples of widespread popular consultation during the conception of great processes of social transformation, usually associated with Party congresses. The greatest weakness has been associated with the lack of effective mechanisms for the public to follow and assess the results. The real consensus achieved in the preparations for the Sixth Congress has been losing strength and could unravel in the absence of a continuing national dialogue that contrasts the real impacts of policies with their declared goals, and that offers effective participation in decisions.

Notes

1. The Junta Central de Planificación (JUCEPLAN) was created by Law 757 of March 11, 1960, a date celebrated annually in Cuba as Planning Day.
2. Years later JUCEPLAN was reorganized and began to operate as the Ministry of Planning. Led from 1964 to 1976 by President of the Republic Osvaldo Dorticós, from 1976 onward it was headed by one of the vice-presidents of the Executive Committee of the Council of Ministers. Finally, in April 1994, it became the Ministry of Economics and Planning.
3. Prominent among them were Michael Kalecki of Poland, Jacques Chonchol of Chile, Juan F. Noyola of Mexico, and Charles Bettelheim of France. Others, such as the Chileans Jaime Barrios, Alban Lataste, and Alberto Martínez played an important practical role in JUCEPLAN as directors or advisors at the national level. Professor Wassily Leontief also visited Havana in 1969, in the context of the construction of an Input-Output Matrix.
4. In 1959 a process of abrupt suppression of private capital began. By 1963, key sectors such as banking, foreign trade, and wholesale commerce were 100 percent state capital. In 1968 the so-called Revolutionary Offensive completely eliminated small-scale retail commerce. Nearly every entity that hired labor succumbed to the wave of nationalizations. Growth of the state sector continued and in 1989 it employed 95 percent of all Cuban workers. Later, in the 1990s, a cautious opening to individual private businesses and to foreign capital emerged, and the conversion of state agricultural enterprises to cooperatives was encouraged.
5. In 1949, as a reaction to the Marshall Plan, many socialist countries of Eastern Europe created an international cooperation network called the Council for Mutual Economic Aid, which took specific legal form ten years after. It later incorporated other countries under socialist aegis such as Vietnam and Cuba.
6. In fact, it was most similar to the USSR model before the 1965 reform; the pre-reform model was more restrictive.
7. Material balances have been the most widely used technique in the so-called planned economies, with the goal of aligning production demands with social needs. They constitute a grouping of many and diverse balances that assign the possible sources and uses of all available and/or necessary resources, trying to capture all the interdependencies in the productive processes. This requires processing great volumes of information about production functions of varied economic units as well as their inventory situations. It also assumes precise knowledge of demand.
8. In this chapter, "market" does not necessarily mean a context in which private producers predominate, nor does the existence of a market require ending all state intervention, for instance in regulating prices. Here "market" refers to a mechanism to allocate resources according to which the economic agents involved are free to make decisions about production, sales, and consumption, given the real existence of alternative options

among which to choose. A reduction in such options would mean a reduction of the market.

9. An example is the signing in 1992 of the Cuban Democracy Act (also known as the Torricelli Act) that banned transactions with Cuba or Cuban citizens on the part of third-country subsidiaries of U.S. companies; among other constraints, it also barred third-country ships that touched Cuban ports from entering U.S. territory for the following 180 days. Later, in 1996, the Cuban Liberty and Democratic Solidarity Act (also known as Helms-Burton) sought to discourage and interfere with foreign investment and to internationalize the blockade. It codified the provisions of that blockade, limited the President's ability to end that policy, and broadened its extraterritorial reach. It denied entrance to the United States to executives of foreign businesses (and their families) that invested in properties that had been confiscated in Cuba, and it established the possibility of suing Cuba in U.S. courts.

10. This period, known in Cuba as the "Battle of Ideas," was characterized by systematic calls for massive political mobilization to demand, initially, that the child Elián González's return to Cuba, and later to confront the harsher interventionist rhetoric and extraterritorial measures of the George W. Bush administration.

11. For example, the Treasury Department's Office of Foreign Assets Control (OFAC) imposed fines of several million dollars on several international entities, including the Dutch bank ABN Amro and PNB Paribas of France (MINREX 2010, 2015).

12. Losses from sixteen hurricanes between 1998 and 2008 were estimated at $20,564 billion (PCC 2011).

13. Trade and financial relations with other countries increased substantially, particularly with China, Vietnam, Russia, Angola, Brazil, and Algeria.

14. Guidelines 1 and 2 from the Sixth Party Congress declared: "The socialist planning system will continue to be the main national management tool of the national economy. Its methodology and organization and control must be modified. Economic planning will [exercise] influence on the market and take into account its characteristics [...] and will encompass all forms of property and management" (PCC 2011).

15. This conception has been congruent with the system's obvious need to suppress any vestige of the market. Further, the goal of assigning resources from the perspective of use value—that is, in response to social needs and not effective demand—had seemed a theoretical and practical possibility in earlier contexts.

16. A brief anecdote will serve to illustrate the level of detail encompassed by Cuban planning. In March 2017, during the process of Municipal Assembly delegates' rendering of accounts to local voters, a delegate from one municipality of Havana informed his voters that this year's plan had assigned to his district (three thousand inhabitants) a total of four demolitions and five structural reinforcements of buildings in danger of collapsing, one stairway repair, and two water pumps for multi-family buildings.

17. A more extensive discussion of this issue may be found in Fernández 2016.
18. An aspect of this issue deserving separate treatment is the problem of over-valuing the CUP within the enterprise sector, which generates perverse incentives and implicit subsidization of import enterprises by export ones. If there were no dual currency and exchange system, this overvaluation would be a problem in its own right. The 1:1 exchange rate of Cuban pesos and U.S. dollars has existed since the post-World War II international regime of exchange rates was established at Bretton Woods in 1944.
19. At first this was a controlled floating exchange rate, with the rate dropping to 1 USD = 18 CUP at the peso's point of maximum appreciation. After 2001, the impact of the destruction of the New York Twin Towers on remittances and tourism, alongside a domestic speculative spiral, led the authorities to fix the rate at 1:27. In 2005, it was revalued to the current rate of 1 USD = 25 CUP.
20. In those years, the hardening of U.S. sanctions made it extraordinarily difficult for Cuba to use dollars for any sort of transaction, which led Cuban authorities to change the denomination of reserves, eliminate the dollar from circulation, replace it with the CUC, and impose a 10% tax on the purchase of dollars with cash. In April 2005, the CUC was revalued at 1 CUC = 1.08 USD. In 2011 the 1:1 rate was restored.
21. The reference is to prices of final goods and services, but also to others such as wages, interest rates, exchange rates, land values, wholesale markets, and specific markets such as that for real estate, motor vehicles, etc.
22. The prices that enterprises pay for fuel and electricity do not constitute a constraint for them and do not reflect the tensions these generate in the balance of payments. The signal perceived by the managers is a mechanism of physical constraint, over which they constantly negotiate and argue against.
23. This does not mean that currency unification would suffice to eliminate such mediations, but it would at least create the conditions for reducing them significantly.
24. The National Development Plan (PCC 2016b) contains references to a number of important concepts with impacts on public administration, such as the emphasis on real citizen participation (paragraphs 43, 53, 188, 189, 214), the need for rules to take priority over discretionality (paragraphs 50, 51, 69, 71, 193), and the urgency of rendering account via evaluation of impacts (paragraphs 10, 52, 62, 63).
25. Between 2009 and 2014 the economy grew at an average rate of 2.4 percent (ONEI 2015).
26. In general, concentration of high market shares is an undesirable phenomenon in any context. It is worse if it results not from economic processes but from political decisions.
27. Cuba has had many, many examples of enterprise ineffectiveness and even errors with substantial impacts on the final consumer, including some reflected in media reports. The fundamental cause lies in their artificial but absolute control over the market and the consequent lack of competition, as well as

the absence of proper incentives within these enterprises (e.g., ETECSA's cell phone services, the Post Office, the Transmetro bus enterprise, and others).
28. An emblematic case a few decades past was the creation of a monopoly on first-class hotels that the Cuban government conceded to Sol-Meliá, as counterproductive as it was unnecessary, which only now is beginning to change.

Bibliography

Brus, Wlodzimierz. 1960. *El funcionamiento de la economía socialista: Problemas generales.* Barcelona: Oikos Ediciones.

Elson, Diana. 1988. "¿Socialismo de mercado o socializando el mercado? La crisis de la economía soviética y el debate mercado/planificación." http://www.cefyl.org.ar.

Espina, Mayra, José Luis Rodríguez, Juan Triana, and Rafael Hernández. 2011. "El Período Especial veinte años después." In *Revista Temas* 65: 59–75.

Fernández Estrada, O. 2011. "El modelo de funcionamiento económico en Cuba y sus transformaciones. Seis ejes articuladores para su análisis. In *Observatorio de la Economía Latinoamericana* 153.

———. 2016. "Hacia una nueva visión de la planificación en Cuba." In *Cuban Studies* 44: 90–111.

JUCEPLAN. 1985. *Apuntes históricos de la Junta Central de Planificación, Tomo I, Esfera Estatal.* Havana: Editora JUCEPLAN.

Mandel, Ernest. 1986. "En defensa de la planificación socialista. La crisis de la economía soviética y el debate mercado/planificación." 1986. http://www.cefyl.org.ar.

Martín, Juan. 2005. *Funciones básicas de la planificación económica y social.* Santiago de Chile: Instituto Latinoamericano y del Caribe de Planificación Económica y Social.

MEP (Ministerio de Economía y Planificación). 2015. "Presentación a la Asamblea Nacional del Poder Popular." Havana, June.

Ministerio de Justicia. 2014. *Gaceta Extraordinaria No. 21, Gaceta Oficial de la República de Cuba.* http://www.gacetaoficial.cu.

———. 2003. "Constitución de la República de Cuba." In *Gaceta Extraordinaria, No 3, Gaceta Oficial de la República de Cuba.* http://www.gacetaoficial.cu.

Ministerio de Relaciones Exteriores. 2010. "Sobre la resolución 65/6 de la Asamblea General de las Naciones Unidas, titulada 'Necesidad de poner fin al bloqueo económico, comercial y financiero impuesto por los Estados Unidos de América contra Cuba.'" June. http://www.prensa-latina.cu/Dossiers/informe-BloqueoEspanol.pdf.

Murillo, Marino. 2013. "Intervención ante la Asamblea Nacional del Poder Popular." Televised speech, Havana, 22 June.

Nove, Alec. 1987. *La economía del socialismo factible.* Madrid: Editorial Pablo Iglesias.

Oficina Nacional de Estadísticas e Información. 2014. "Informe sobre organización institucional." http://www.onei.cu.

Ollman, Bertell, David Schweickart, James Lawler, and Hillel Ticktin. 1998. *Market Socialism. The Debate among Socialists.* New York: Routledge.

PCC (Partido Comunista de Cuba). 1997. *Resolución Económica del V Congreso del PCC.* Havana, April.

———. 2011. *Lineamientos de la política económica y social del Partido y la Revolución.*" Havana, Sixth Congress of the Cuban Communist Party, April 18.

———. 2016a. *Actualización de los Lineamientos de la política económica y social del Partido y la Revolución para el período 2016–2021.* Havana, Seventh Congress of the Cuban Communist Party, April.

———. 2016b. *Plan Nacional de Desarrollo Económico y Social hasta 2030: Propuesta de Visión de la Nación, Ejes y Sectores Estratégicos.* Havana, Seventh Congress of the Cuban Communist Party, April.

Rodríguez, Carlos Rafael. 1980. "Problemas prácticos de la planificación centralizada." In *Revista Comercio Exterior de México* 30:11, 1214–1219.

4

Small and Medium-Sized Enterprises in Cuba: A Necessary Step

Omar Everleny Pérez Villanueva

Introduction

Worldwide, there is steadily growing interest in the current or optimal place of micro, small, and medium-sized businesses in economic development processes. In many countries, these enterprises, known in Spanish by the acronym MPYMES, dominate industry and services. In contrast to large enterprises, the size of MPYMES allows them to be more flexible and to adapt better to their environments.

The rise of inter-sectoral subcontracting and cooperation has contributed to the reactivation and dynamism of many economies in the world, including those of developed countries. Production chains grow up around manufacturing of parts, components, and equipment, or around joint implementation of projects and designs; these chains include many small businesses with links to large companies.

The role of such small or medium-sized enterprises in job creation, market activation, improved income distribution, regional development, and more flexible adaptation to economic crises is indisputable. Their use of labor power is generally more intensive where capital is scarce; they also utilize more local resources, which ties them tightly to regional and local economies.

This chapter offers readers a vision of the important contributions of the creation of small and medium-sized businesses to the emergence of a fully articulated network of enterprises in a country like Cuba. This is not a novelty in Cuban economic reality because micro, small, and medium-sized businesses were the prevailing reality before 1959. Therefore I will briefly discuss the general elements of these enterprises, then their historical evolution up to the present day, and finally some proposals for implementation.

General Description of MPYMES

One obstacle to discussion of MPYMES is their definition, including quantitative distinctions among small, medium, and large enterprises in terms of the number of employees. A business with twenty-five employees is large within the sector of domestic services such as hairdressing or food preparation, but very small in terms of the chemical or pharmaceutical industries. Within the knowledge economy (software, Internet, etc.), new enterprises have always begun with few employees. Even those entities that now occupy the international heights of this sector began as micro-enterprises, among which the most famous examples are Apple, Microsoft, Facebook, Amazon, and Google.

Enterprises may be classified as micro, small, medium, or large, but any proposed definition brings difficulties because even in the current business world there is no consensus, and definitions tend to be arbitrary. Among the criteria utilized are numbers of employees, sales volume, enterprise capital, or combinations of these. Internationally, especially in Europe and particularly in Spain, the number of employees is the most frequently used criterion; the assumption is that a micro enterprise is one with up to ten workers, a small business has eleven to forty-nine, a medium from fifty to 249, and a large enterprise has 250 or more employees. However, this usage may vary from country to country, and even within a given country. For example, CEPAL's study (1993) (United Nations Economic Commission for Latin America and the Caribbean) offered a classification scheme that defined micro enterprises as having one to four employees; small ones, five to nineteen; and medium, between twenty and forty-nine.

The category of small and medium-sized enterprises is internationally known by the Spanish acronym PYMES.[1] MPYMES is an expansion of the original to include micro enterprises. Elements to take into account depend on the regulations and goals of each country, given the lack of agreement on what criteria should be used to measure enterprise size or which dimensions are the most appropriate.[2]

MPYMES include a great variety of businesses, from traditional artisans, street vendors, and repair shops to manufacturers of construction and industrial materials, among others. They are also very common in the sector of recycling paper, cardboard, iron, and other materials. An important part of MPYMES output consists of cheap consumer goods, often destined for the domestic market; this also favors the use of local raw materials.

Economists Monreal, Carranza, and Gutiérrez (1997) discussed the relation between productive efficiency and forms of property, showing that large private enterprises and some medium-sized ones develop a separation of property and control according to the nature of the economic activities they undertake and their need for large capital inputs. However, for small enterprises and many of the medium ones, those that do not require mobilization of great amounts of capital given the nature of their specific activities, scale, and complexity of production, this separation is unnecessary and even counterproductive.

For a country's economy to prosper, it must be capable of producing riches. Regardless of the dominant economic system, enterprises are the entities responsible for making this happen. To fulfill its productive function, an enterprise must be able to utilize the factors of production such as work (human resources) and capital (money and all it can acquire: machinery, equipment, tools, buildings, etc.). Another no less important factor is organization (administration or direction of the enterprise); it coordinates the above factors to achieve given objectives or goals, which constitute the *raison d'être* of the enterprise (Arredondo, 2012).

Beyond being an economic unit, the enterprise is also a social entity, embedded in the society it serves, from which it cannot remain apart. The society must offer it order guaranteed by law and public power; a labor force and consumers; the education of its workers, technicians, and managers; and means of communication and economic infrastructure. Since the enterprise receives so much from society, there is an inevitable interdependence between the two. Thus, economic goals should not be placed above social goals; rather, the aim should be to try to achieve both without detriment or short change to either.

In Cuba, MPYMES can be a test laboratory for people with entrepreneurial ambitions, a place for them to manage a small enterprise where leaders may demonstrate their managerial skills in a healthy way. Still, it is evident that there is a high quotient of personal risk; not every individual will triumph, and the mortality statistics for this type of enterprise are high.

In order for MPYMES in Cuba to be put to appropriate use and develop their due importance, the government must contribute to their linkage with larger-scale industry, especially in the state sector, offering the necessary support and creating institutions that will contribute to their growth. These include specialized banks or micro-credit institutions. This will happen only if the Cuban state gives the MPYMES room for action and sees them as necessary elements rather than as competitors; that is, they can succeed only if the state acts in good faith or, amounting to the same thing, if it offers them support rather than control them in bad faith.

Description of MPYMES in Cuba

Discussing MPYMES in Cuba requires a brief review of the country's experience before and after the Revolution. In 1954, when Cuba had some 2,300 industrial enterprises, two-thirds of its factories employed fewer than ten workers. The sugar industry was made up of a group of large mills accounting for a significant share of production, plus a great number of small mills. The rest of domestic industry was made up principally of small plants with low capital investment and few employees, producing primarily for the domestic market.[3]

However, in the course of the 1950s an important group of transnational companies sought opportunities in Cuba, beginning a process of investment that grew to represent a third of the total. Most significant among these companies were electric utilities, petroleum refineries, and factories producing tires, paint, nickel, milled flour, detergents, bottles, and plate glass. Domestic investors with access to bank loans invested in steel mills, cement factories, and construction materials, diversifying so as not to rely only on sugar production. In spite of these new larger companies, micro enterprises still represented 45 percent of the Cuban enterprise fabric, while small ones made up an estimated 35.5 percent.

Beginning in 1959, the laws and transformations of the revolutionary period featured the nationalizations carried out mostly in 1960. Thereafter, transnational enterprise investments stopped while the confrontation with the United States sharpened. In this context, the importance of the state sector as measured by the value of durable capital goods varied in proportion to the advance of nationalization; by 1968 most enterprises were state-owned outside of the agricultural sector.

In 1968, the state also nationalized the entire small private retail, service, and industrial sectors, a move that brought state activity practically down to the street-vendor level, provoking a total change in the economic structure of the country. From then on, the economy was characterized by the predominance of the state sector in all branches, with only a tiny private sector remaining in transport and agriculture.

The state's investment policy between 1970 and 1990 sought to increase industrial employment and production. This tended to create large enterprises with vertically integrated production complexes. One result was to limit inter-enterprise cooperation and the full exploitation of installed capacity, eliminating both competition and cooperation among smaller firms. The preference was to take advantage of so-called economies of scale of larger enterprises, a path followed also by most countries in Eastern

Europe and the Soviet Union. However, this also provoked the growth of an exaggerated and inevitable bureaucracy, and lack of incentive for improvement provided by competition.

In 1988, 88 percent of Cuba's enterprises could be classified as large, with a range of 251 to 1,000 employees; the rest were medium or small, but with workforces still larger than international averages. Cuba followed an extensive-growth model, that is, production increases stemmed not from improved efficiency but rather from adding factors of production such as more land, more workers, or more factories.

After 1989, with the exhaustion of the extensive model of the Cuban economy and also the breakup of the socialist bloc, the economy entered a deep crisis, with a large two-digit drop in imports that provoked partial paralysis of industrial sectors or factories; at certain moments, capacity utilization dropped to less than 20 percent.

The country began to introduce survival measures. Large inefficient state farms, now lacking imported inputs, became instead Basic Units of Cooperative Production (Spanish initials UBPC). Some four hundred such large farms were converted into four thousand UBPCs. Also, in order to increase the supply of some basic consumer services, create new employment options, and move toward the legalization of a growing number of underground-economy workers, the state legislated Decree Law 141/93 that allowed certain options for self-employment (*trabajo por cuenta propia*, Spanish initials TCP). The state also issued new regulations determining who was permitted to engage in such self-employment and established requirements for the operation of all TCPs.

In effect, the government accessed internal reserves that existed in the country; this led it to open up TCP opportunities in 1993. This move created the conditions for shifts in the importance of some employment sectors such as food services (where private restaurants popularly known as *paladares* were created but at that time were limited to twelve seats), which opened the doors to a reemergence of Cuban micro-enterprise. However, these micro-enterprises proved very difficult to control, although fines were imposed on a selective basis so as to convey the message that the state would not tolerate failure to comply with regulations.

Other industries in the 1990s underwent significant change. Some closed while others reduced the number of working shifts, yet in general large enterprises continued to predominate. Only in certain high-value-added sectors such as biotechnology were small factories introduced, with small staffs and much more flexible operations to make certain products like vaccines.

Figure 4.1: Licenses Granted to Self-Employed Workers (Thousands)

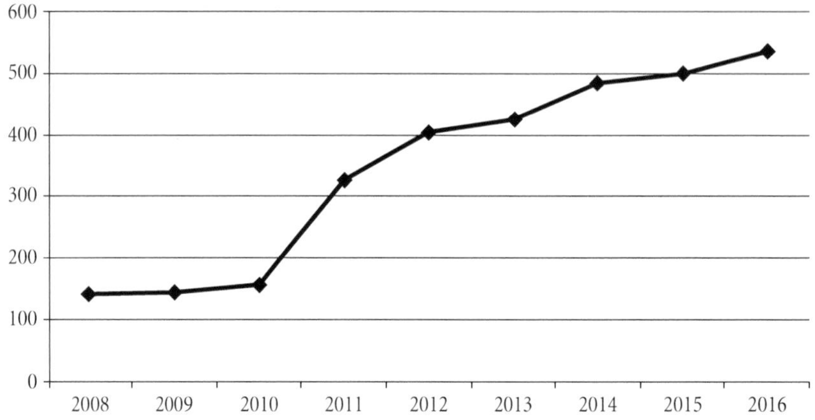

Source: Constructed by the author on the basis of varied sources including ONEI, *Anuario Estadístico de Cuba*, and *Granma* official newspaper, Havana, Cuba.

With this opening of the Cuban economy in the 1990s, the number of licensed private workers grew to 121,000 in 1994 and reached a peak of 165,000 in 2005, which was then followed by a "significant" decrease.[4] With the inauguration of Raúl Castro as the country's president and as part of the process of restructuring the national economy given its difficult circumstances, Resolution 32 of October 2010 relaunched the private sector. At that time, the number of permitted activities rose from 157 to 178, and then to 201 in 2012. Many regulations were loosened in order to stimulate the small private sector's activity: self-employed persons were now allowed to hire employees, receive credits, open bank accounts (though in practice this has not become prevalent), and establish relations with the state sector through contracts, among other changes. The cap of twelve seats on private restaurants was also lifted. In this situation, the "new self-employed" may really be considered private micro and small businesses.

Between 2008 and 2015, President Raúl Castro's administration undertook very far-reaching changes. Among the most outstanding are the growth of the private and cooperative sector, new directives to deregulate Cuban state enterprises, and the granting of usufruct rights to all who want to work the land. This made room for the creation of many MPYMES, rendering Cuba more similar to its counterparts in the rest of the world, although it is important to recognize that approved legislation is one thing and implementation of the new laws is another—creating thereby the impression that regulations are issued but not put into effect.

Figure 4.1 shows the sustained rise in the number of licenses granted for private work, with a takeoff point after 2010. The 535,000 licenses as of the end of December 2016[5] represent an increase of 378,000 compared to 2010. While there have been certain monthly oscillations, the final figures for each year (on which the graph is based) show an increase from the previous one. Although the rhythm of new license approvals has slowed in comparison to 2011 and 2012, the upward trend continues.

Current Issues Regarding MPYMES

The state continues to use the official term "self-employed workers" but, in practice, given fewer restrictions on this kind of activity, these economic agents are now operating in the territory of micro and small private businesses. Still, some additional reformulations of important concepts and necessary limits are required to adapt the "rules of the game" to all economic actors. This is expected to occur as part of the elaboration of the theoretical conception of the Cuban economic model, an issue mentioned by President Raúl Castro at the close of the National Assembly meetings in December 2012. Subsequently, in his main report to the Seventh Congress of the Cuban Communist Party in April 2016, the First Secretary referred to ". . . calling things by their name and not hiding behind illogical euphemisms to mask reality. The increase in self-employment and the authorization to contract a workforce has led in practice to the existence of medium, small and micro private enterprises which today operate without proper legal status."

This same Congress also issued a document called the "Conceptualization of the Economic and Social Model of Socialist Development." Its paragraphs 180–182 discuss the need to create MPYMES.

Paragraph 180: Cuban persons may create the following types of activities:
Paragraph 181:1. Small businesses carried out fundamentally by the worker and his or her family.
Paragraph 182: 2. Private enterprises of medium, small, and micro scale, according to their volume of activity and number of workers, [which are] recognized as legal persons [entities].

So it is evident that the government has begun discussions on MPYMES, which would be central to the process of developing of the Cuban economy.

Palenzuela and Sacchetti (2007) have pointed out how self-employment activities, initially a subsistence option for domestic groups in Cuba, soon grew in complexity and specialization to the point of sometimes achieving highly structured work relations and division of labor. According to these authors, such entities became micro-enterprises utilizing strategies of savings, accumulation, and particular forms of investment and capitalization, all within the (narrow) limits permitted by the government. In such micro-enterprises, the owner of the license was assisted by paid workers in numbers varying according to the type of work (from a minimum of one to more than ten). At that time all such employees were in irregular positions with regard to the law, which did not recognize their existence, a gap later overcome by the country's current legislation. In other words, in the 1990s there were already persons who could be called micro and small business entrepreneurs, running well-organized businesses with enterprise structures, even if they remained "hidden" by virtue of their illegal character. Medium-size private business would emerge in the future once other activities were lawfully authorized.

Thus, today's Cuba should reconceptualize the term "self-employment" because it does not cover a large share of the economic units that currently operate. Because of their capacity to mobilize productive factors (capital and human resources) in an organized way, they can be considered enterprises, fitting thereby into the definition discussed above. Despite the long time during which the process of "flexibilization" of regulations has unfolded, this type of employment is still in its infancy. It remains difficult to see its true reach and potential, given the precariousness of the economic environment in which it is developing, the gradual pace of changes in the regulatory framework, and the difficulties with inputs, among others. Yet there is no doubt that today's "*cuentapropistas*" have evolved, and they need only time to demonstrate their potential.

Taking into account the concepts utilized so far, the transformations that have taken place in Cuba since the process of expanding self-employment began, the literature consulted, and the reality in which the sector operates, it is appropriate to replace the concept of the "self-employed" with that of the micro and small enterprise (MPYME); this classification can cover and be adapted to the whole universe to which it refers.[6] Those holding the licenses, in turn, can be called entrepreneurs.

Some believe that the majority of Cuban industry, at least in light manufacturing and some other branches, could become MPYMES, which would reshape Cuba's tattered domestic industrial base. It is undeniable that such MPYMES can count on very important advantages in Cuba, such as a highly qualified workforce and a market with high unmet demand. Indeed, Cuba surpasses the necessary conditions for MPYMES to form part of the engine of economic growth, linked with larger industrial units as needed.

The factor of local development is also favorable to the creation of MPYMES. In an archipelago of nearly 110,000 square kilometers with eleven million inhabitants, locating large enterprises in small urban settlements is problematic; these enterprises do best in cities with 100,000 or more inhabitants. Small factories, on the other hand, help to transform the productive and occupational profile of less dense areas and to diminish migratory flows toward denser urban areas or places that offer better prospects from prioritized sectors such as tourism, mining, and others.

An MPYME has to be linked with the entire surrounding structure of enterprises, which must be designed and managed in such a way that shows that the state recognizes the role of the MPYME and creates the necessary conditions to take advantage of its full potential. It would be appropriate for the emerging non-state sector, which can become a dense fabric of MPYMES over the medium term, to be able to open bank accounts and employ the payroll instruments common in banking practice. This is currently a complex and cumbersome process, yet if well run it would have positive effects: it would diminish operating costs and reduce the risk of accumulating and managing excessive volumes of cash (via banks accounts, the MPYMES could pay their taxes, social security contributions, and utility bills); begin to create financially viable ties with state enterprises and the institutional structure, while facilitating interrelations and the formation of value chains within the private and cooperative sector itself; and facilitate compliance with the law, especially in reducing tax evasion (if, for instance, all businesses with gross income exceeding 50,000 CUP were required to use bank accounts). MPYMES would have an incentive to deposit their revenues in such accounts because they would constitute their collateral for soliciting loans, among other benefits (Vidal, 2012).

Before Decree-Law 289 (offering credit to *cuentapropistas*) went into effect at the end of 2011, MPYMES had already doubled their pre-2010 numbers while remaining completely outside the formal banking network. By 2016 there were 535,000 licenses issued, with the sector having very few links to formal financing. It may be assumed, therefore, that the investments and working capital of the new businesses have come from the savings of the self-employed and micro-entrepreneurs themselves, from remittances received from outside the country, and resources that move through informal financial channels (such as loans from relatives, friends, or other individuals). In some cases, the capital and the businesses even belong to foreigners, often Cuban-Americans who use resident Cuban citizens as cover.

Central Bank statistics reveal that in the Banco Metropolitano, which operates solely in Havana, only 1 percent of the 2015 loan portfolio was issued to small farmers, urban cooperatives, and the self-employed; in 2015, only 5,908 checking accounts had been opened by self-employed workers.[7] In other banks such as BANDEC, only 6 percent of the loan portfolio went to urban cooperatives, self-employed workers, and individuals purchasing construction materials or electric cooking equipment. In the Banco Popular de Ahorro, only 5 percent of loans went to urban cooperatives, self-employed workers, individuals purchasing construction materials or electric cooking equipment, and individual farmers. In short, Cuba's state banking system plays a minuscule role in the current financing of MPYMES. This has to change.

MPYMES are not a new topic in discussion and debate about the Cuban economy. In 1997, at the request of the Ministry of Economics and Planning, a policy paper on the implementation of MPYMES in the country was prepared by the Centro de Estudios de la Economía Cubana (CEEC) together with the Ministry of Finance and Prices, the Banco Popular de Ahorro, and the Centro de Investigación de la Economía Mundial.[8] Recommendations included a general one to create this type of enterprise, a series of steps to be taken in this regard, the institutions it would be necessary to create, and a summary of the various economic measures already taken that could favor this type of enterprise, such as the shrinking of the country's industrial sector, the transformation of the farm sector, the development and expansion of self-employment, the development of local and regional economies, and the new role of joint ventures with foreign capital, among others.

Also in the mid-1990s, a group of Cuban officials led by Rafael Alhama and Juan Jose Pérez of the Centro de Investigación del Trabajo (a division of the Ministry of Work and Social Security) put forward a scheme of the modalities of MPYMES in Cuba, including:

1. State PYME (a new sector, with elements of decentralization and deconcentration of large enterprises).
2. Cooperative PYME (offering a greater possibility of service, commerce, transport, and agricultural activity).
3. Micro-enterprise (created by way of the approved activities for self-employment).[9]

Other variants of forms of property include state firms, cooperatives, private firms, and combinations of these. To them may be added mixed enterprises, not only in the current sense of those linking foreign capital and domestic state capital, but also variants such as an arrangement allowing foreign capital to associate with private domestic capital. One path to explore would be the sale of shares to workers, or the supply of some means of production; this variant seems best for the fashion industry and for service sectors.

In a general sense, Cuban MPYMEs could bring many advantages, but the enterprises so created would need to have the autonomy and operational room that characterize them at a world level; the socialist planning of the Economic Ministry should not conspire against their functioning. Enterprises should operate under new conceptions of administration and management covering everything from product design, acquisition of means of production, product quality assurance to encourage competitiveness, and growing levels of personalization of attention to consumers, among others.

One issue regarding small private property that raises concerns for Cuba's policy makers is the reappearance of social inequality since the start of transformations in the 1990s. However, the growth in self-employment was not the only factor stimulating this phenomenon, even though revenues in this sector are in general comparatively high. The other factor was the near-freezing of salaries of Cuban workers and retirees. This has contributed to a paralysis of state workers' standard of living, with these workers finding themselves at a great disadvantage with respect to private ones. But the remedy is not to punish the private winners but rather to consider and propose alternatives to increase the incentives of state workers.

In 1996, in its internal working document about the value of considering small and middle-sized enterprises as a higher phase of the incipient self-employment sector, the Ministry of Economics and Planning warned:

> . . . There is a psychological and contradictory fact that influences, though it does not determine, the behavior of the variable. This is associated with the low political acceptance of people carrying out this type of work, which needs to be changed . . . therefore what is needed is a form of indirect regulation that allows for more effective monitoring of this activity, such as:
>
> 1. Creation of a market for inputs, with sufficient suppliers so as to be methodologically subordinate to MINCIN [Ministry of Internal Commerce], with a single billing system that allows monitoring and control of the source of the products and the level of retail prices.

2. Establishment competitive pricing—that is, wholesale prices for inputs that are sold in that market, which should in all cases allow for covering the costs incurred in their production and also should be sufficiently low to discourage their diversion to other markets.

3. Encouragement of payment procedures through the national banking system to allow greater and wider transfer of the activities of this sector.[10]

Alas, almost twenty years later the same concerns about the development of the MPYMES persist. Because of Cuba's peculiarities, the categorization of MPYMES according to the number of workers, based on the international literature and structure of the Cuban enterprise in the mid-20th century, might show very little change today.

Since Cuba's published statistics do not tally the sales of micro or small business—in other words, there is no value data—and given the distortions brought by Cuba's dual-currency system—any ranking by size has to make use of number of workers as the indicator. However, in an economy such as Cuba's where knowledge is the most abundant resource, this criterion should be supplemented by that of enterprise size, including sales, resources, etc. The challenge is to create an information system that will compile such statistics. For the time being, the activities already approved in the current regulations regarding so-called self-employment and urban cooperatives could be utilized to experiment with new classificatory categories.

Table 4.1: Micro-, Small-, and Medium Enterprises by Economic Sector According to the Number of Workers

	Industry	Commerce and Services
Micro-enterprises	5	3
Small enterprises	20	10
Medium enterprises (lower stratum)	21–30	20
Medium enterprises (upper stratum)	21–50	30

Source: Constructed by the author on the basis of studies commissioned by the Ministry of Economics and Planning to the CEEC and other institutions in 1996.

Another issue that deserves consideration is how best to utilize Cuba's highly educated workforce, that is, how to prioritize enterprises that make greater use of knowledge, which would avoid the loss of skilled human resources to sectors offering higher incomes in lower-skilled jobs. It would also put a brake on emigration both to countries with a greater level of development than Cuba's and also to less developed countries in Latin America where the social pyramid is not as inverted as in Cuba. Cuba could expect many good results to flow from this type of enterprises, especially those that contribute toward the desired achievement of a more homogeneous economic and social development in various geographic regions.

In November 2015, at seminar at the University of Havana, an outstanding business scholar Michael Chu from the Harvard Business School commented that if the Cuban state was interested in developing knowledge-based enterprises, it should promote the birth of many MPYMES, facilitate their development, and not punish them—especially the honest ones that demonstrate the results of their labor. The eminent professor was quite correct.

Yet barely six months after his remarks, Cuban policy retreated. The intent was to reorganize the operations of the incipient MPYMES, but the measures taken have placed roadblocks on the path of the most successful entrepreneurs. These roadblocks have ranged from closing businesses, imposing fines and confiscations, and demanding receipts for purchases, to freezing new licenses in the food service sector; by early 2017, however, this climate of antagonism seemed diminished.

Another alert comes from sociologists, philosophers, journalists, and writers on the topic of the social inequality that has been growing in contemporary Cuba, some of whom relate this inequality to the emergence of a new social class created by the new entrepreneurs. They are correct to observe that one part of the society is not advancing and that real gaps have been created. However, the cause is not that one part has advanced, but that the state has not permitted all citizens to advance at the same rate. The salaries of state-budgeted enterprises are insufficient, and pensions are at a subsistence level, among other issues.

Final Elements to Consider

The activities authorized for self-employment remain insufficient to make use of Cuba's professional potential. This is true even though the workers who now have these licenses can see improvements in their standard of living and are offering useful services to the populace and the state.

Economic history offers many cases of large businesses that began as micro-enterprises, many of which progressed with little financial aid because the outstanding factor was the human talent of their creators. Apple, Microsoft, and Facebook are but three instances out of many.

Cuba needs to create an institution whose fundamental mission is the development of MPYMES through a system of "one-stop shopping" that maintains ties with the various regions of the country and other pertinent organizations—an autonomous institution that empowers its members, one very different from those known recently.

As practiced in the rest of the world, it would also be useful to create a development bank or other micro-credit financial institutions specializing in serving this segment of the market. Likewise, it might be worth engaging in international collaboration, for instance with Mexico, where micro-credit for the development of micro-enterprises has advanced considerably.

There is a need for legislation to stimulate connections between state enterprises and MPYMES, so the latter could participate in some phase of export-oriented production; such small private agents could improve the competitiveness of the final exportable product.

Although Cuban authorities show interest in expanding the MPYMES segment of the Cuban market, as demonstrated in official discourse backed up by numerous concrete actions, the actions remain insufficient. Although they evidently stem from this interest and are part of a stimulus program, they are not yet sufficiently organized or integrally structured to achieve a more rapid advance for this sector, with greater possibilities of enterprise success. A sequence of steps to achieve the results of which these enterprises are capable would look something like this:

1. Broaden the activities that can be authorized for the urban private and cooperative sectors, which form the small business base.
2. Offer credits in sufficient quantity and with less stringent demands as to size of guarantees.
3. Create a wholesale market for inputs.
4. Grant the right to import or export products.

If and when the government understands the positive economic role and potential of this type of enterprise, Cuban MPYMES would become a more viable part of the updating of the economic model and would yield more positive results.

If, on the other hand, MPYMES are regarded more from a political than from an economic angle and policy objectives retain the idea that these enterprises should neither amass wealth nor enlarge their operations, then it is doubtful that the state will opt to develop MPYMES, which explains the absence thus far of the necessary steps for their strengthening and development.

Notes

1. See *Diccionario de la Real Academia Española*, 2001.
2. See Llopis, 2000.
3. Rodríguez, 1980, p. 151.
4. Pérez Villanueva and Vidal, 2011.
5. "Al cierre del 2016 más de 535 mil trabajadores no estatales," *Trabajadores* newspaper, print edition, 9 January 2017.
6. It may be difficult to conceive of an individual carrying out an activity with a very simple level of organization, such as a licensed street vendor selling peanuts, as a micro-enterprise or entrepreneur, but concepts do not discriminate. There is a certain conceptual zone where the categories of the micro-enterprise and the self-employed worker blur and overlap; in such cases it may be more accurate and useful to retain the term "self-employed."
7. Perez Villanueva, Mundul, and Gutiérrez, 2016.
8. Ministerio de Economía y Planificación, 1996.
9. Internal document of the Centro de Investigaciones del Trabajo, Ministerio del Trabajo y la Seguridad Social, 1996.
10. Ministerio de Economía y Planificación, 1996.

Bibliography

Arredondo, Leonardo. 2012. "El trabajo por cuenta propia, la micro y la pequeña empresa en Cuba: Su potencial para el desarrollo económico." Master's thesis, FLACSO Cuba.

CEPAL. 1993. "La pequeña y mediana empresa. Algunos aspectos."

———. 2012. "Experiencias exitosas en innovación, inserción internacional e inclusión social. Una mirada desde las PYMES." September 2011. Consulted 20 November 2012 at http://www.eleconomista.cubaweb.cu/2011/nro410 /estrategias.html.

Diccionario de la Real Academia Española, Ed. XXII. 2001.

Llopis, Francisco. 2000. "Análisis de la iniciativa empresarial de la pequeña empresa: incorporación del enfoque estratégico al proceso de creación." Doctoral thesis, Universidad de Alicante, Spain.

Marcelo, Luis, and Oscar U. Echevarría. 1999. "El mayor problema de las PYMES: su propio tamaño." In *Cuba: Investigación Económica* 5:2.

Ministerio de Economía y Planificación. 1996. "Las PYMES no estatales en el proceso de transformación de la economía cubana." Unpublished paper circulated among internal working group members.

Monreal, Pedro, Julio Carranza, and Luis Gutiérrez. 1997. "La pequeña y mediana empresa en Cuba. Aportes para un debate actual." In *Problemas del Desarrollo*, 28:111. Mexico City.

Palenzuela, Pablo, and Elena Sacchetti. 2007. "El trabajo por cuenta propia en Cuba: un espacio para nuevas culturas del trabajo." In *Sociología del Trabajo*, nueva época, 59 (Spring).

Partido Comunista de Cuba. 2016a. Central Report to the 7th Congress of the Communist Party of Cuba, English translation published in *Granma* 18 April, consulted 30 January 2017 at http://en.granma.cu/cuba/2016-04-18/the-development -of-the-national-economy-along-with-the-struggle-for-peace-and-our -ideological-resolve-constitute-the-partys-principal-missions.

———. 2016b. "Conceptualización del modelo económico y social cubano de desarrollo socialista." Tabloid edition of *Granma* newspaper, Havana, April.

Pérez Villanueva, Omar Everleny. 1995. "Las PYMES en el contexto internacional." Havana: Centro de Estudios de la Economía Cubana.

Pérez Villanueva, Omar Everleny, and Viviana Togores. 1996. "La pequeña y mediana empresa en Cuba: Viabilidad o utopía." Havana: Centro de Estudios de la Economía Cubana.

Pérez, Everleny, and Pavel Vidal. 2010. "Entre el ajuste fiscal y los cambios estructurales, se extiende el cuentapropismo." *Boletín cuatrimestral*, CEEC.

———. 2012. "El trabajo por cuenta propia y sus limitaciones para la producción." September, 2011. Consulted 10 November 2012 at http://www.ipscuba.net /index.php?option=com_k2&view=item&id=2158&Itemid=10.

Pérez Villanueva, Omar Everleny. 2015. "PYMES en Cuba: ¿Utopía o realidad necesaria?" In *Miradas a la economía Cubana: Un análisis desde el sector no estatal*, pp. 29–36. Havana: Editorial Caminos.

Pérez Villanueva, Omar Everleny, Jessica León Mundul, and Marlén Sánchez Gutiérrez. 2016. "Fuentes de acumulación para la transformación productiva en Cuba." Paper presented at the annual conference of the Centro de Estudios de la Economía Cubana, April.

Ritter, A., and T. Henken. 2015. *Entrepreneurial Cuba: The Changing Policy Landscape*. Boulder: First Forum Press.

Rodríguez, Gonzalo. 1980. *El proceso de industrialización de la economía cubana.* Havana: Editorial Ciencias Sociales.

Vidal, Pavel. 2012. "La apertura a las microfinanzas en Cuba." In *La economía cubana: ensayos para una reestructuración necesaria.* Havana: Editorial Molinos Trade S.A.

Zabala, María del Carmen, et al. 2015. *Retos para la equidad social en el proceso de actualización del modelo económico Cubano.* Havana: Editorial Ciencias Sociales.

5

The New Cuban Cooperatives: Current Situation and Some Proposals to Improve Performance

Dayrelis Ojeda Suris

Cuba's cooperative movement has grown through the years, with a particular impetus in the agricultural sector after the triumph of the revolution in 1959. These farming cooperatives were the only organizations of that kind from 1959 to May 2013 (ONEI 2013), when the first Non-Agricultural Cooperative (Spanish initials CNA) was created. The CNAs began to develop following the VI Communist Party Congress's approval in 2011 of the Economic and Social Guidelines of the Party and the Revolution, which stated that cooperatives would be one of the non-state enterprise forms to be included within the new economic model to be implemented in the coming years in Cuba.

This chapter seeks to examine these new Cuban cooperatives following the 2016 VII Party Congress, assess their strengths and weaknesses and suggest a few proposals to improve their performance. The chapter begins with a summary of the history of Cuban cooperatives from the colonial period until the approval of the Guidelines in 2011, a discussion of what is meant by a Non-Agricultural Cooperative and its guiding principles, and what must be taken into account when creating one, and it concludes with an analysis of the approval process, showing the ways that CNAs are being created and the main problems that emerge.

The next section focuses on the achievements and difficulties of these cooperatives, based on the opinions of their own members, prospective members, and scholars and researchers—opinions collected through workshops and exchanges in several provinces of the country. The chapter concludes with some proposals to facilitate the development of these new cooperatives within the Cuban economy, entities that have improved the quality of life of their members and their family, created jobs, enabled import substitution, and revived public services that had disappeared in some parts of the country.

Cooperatives in Cuba

In Cuba, references to cooperatives date back to the colonial era because the existence of such associative entities in nineteenth century Spain (Fernández 2005, 59) had made itself felt in the colony. There are also references to the subject during the neocolonial period (1902–1958) (Fernández, 273), but these cooperatives were ephemeral, as they were formed only as means of sheer survival in small and economically marginalized sectors (Fernández, 41). For example, five cooperatives founded in the mid-twentieth century in Cienfuegos survived for an average of four-and-three-quarters years (Fernández, 41). They were:

- Cooperativa Agrícola y de Reparto de Tierra, in the municipality of Aguada de Pasajeros, founded July 18, 1946, and dissolved May 6, 1953; duration six years, ten months.
- Cooperativa de Consumo y Vivienda de Empleados de Las Villas, in the municipality of Cienfuegos, founded November 9, 1950, and dissolved June 22, 1956; duration five years, six months.
- Cooperativa Occidental "Campesinos de la Ciénaga de Zapata," in the municipality of de Aguada de Pasajeros, founded July 12, 1951, and dissolved July 30, 1954; duration three years.
- Cooperativa Campesina "Juncalito la Isla del Barrio de Jagüey Chico," in the municipality of Aguada de Pasajeros, founded July 28, 1957, and dissolved June 29, 1960; duration three years.
- Cooperativa de Transporte "La Conchita," in the municipality of Cienfuegos, founded September 6, 1950, and dissolved May 4 de mayo, 1956; duration five years, seven months.

Other cooperatives were created by influential groups to enrich themselves through corrupt business practices, which led to their dissolution and confiscation of their properties (Fernández, 41), under the provisions of the Law of Associations in force since 1888, a situation that did not give rise to the socialization of a true culture of cooperatives during that era.

The triumph of the revolution brought the development of cooperatives in such production sectors as agriculture, ranching, fishing, charcoal, and yarn, and service and consumer cooperatives known as People's Stores. They reached a total of 485 production cooperatives and 440 consumer cooperatives (Fernández, 43) before the political processes in the early 1960s led to the creation of large state properties instead.

In 1960, the banking institutions that had offered agricultural credit (Banco Fomento Agrícola e Industrial and Compañía Cuban Land) were eliminated, creating the need for a mechanism through which the small tobacco farmers in the province of Pinar del Río could obtain credit; this led to the creation of Credit and Service Cooperatives (Spanish initials CCS) beginning in 1961 (Nova 2011, 322).

These cooperatives were made up of small private farmers who had received land through the agrarian reform, voluntarily joining together to receive benefits such as bank loans, modern technology (otherwise inaccessible because of its cost), and to enter into arrangements about markets and prices and other aspects, while maintaining ownership of their land and working it individually. (Before the CCS there were Peasant Associations created at the beginning of the revolution, which paved the way for later cooperatives.)

After the 1960 sugar harvest, the first Cane Cooperatives were created (Nova, 323) as a means to socialize the farms that had become state property, but a lack of experience with this type of productive organization, low educational levels of the leaders, and lack of carry-over of administrative experience from the pre-revolutionary era led to misuse of resources, as a result of which, after the conclusion of the 1962 harvest, the government decided to convert these cooperatives into state farms.

This period saw also the creation of a type of cooperative called Agricultural Societies, in which members socialized their land ownership and equipment and shared their collective income. Later this experiment was abandoned, but it may be seen as a predecessor of the Agricultural Production Cooperatives (Spanish initials CPA) that emerged in the 1970s (Hernández 2013, 22).

In 1975, the First Congress of the Cuban Communist Party decided to support and develop the cooperative movement as a superior form of production for peasants who had received land in the agrarian reform, by creating the CPA entities (Nova, 324). CPAs are workers' cooperatives, in which small farmers contribute their land to the cooperative and work it in common. Communities were built within these cooperatives, with schools, medical centers, playgrounds, child care centers, social clubs, and other institutions of a social character, thus contributing to improvement of peasants' living conditions.

In the second half of the 1980s, the Cuban economy began to show signs of deterioration in its macroeconomic indicators, leading to a crisis in the early 1990s. This process included the farm sector, characterized mostly by large state enterprises, a high degree of centralization, industrialized agriculture that consumed large quantities of inputs, and an important degree of investment per hectare but with high external dependence (Nova, 325).

As the crisis deepened, it became clear that the existing cooperatives, the CPAs and the CCSs, were better prepared than the state farms to operate under difficult conditions of limited resources: until 1992, 85 percent of the CPAs were profitable, as compared to only 27 percent of the state farms (Nova, 326).

In September 1993, the Political Bureau of the Cuban Communist Party decided to create the Basic Units of the Cooperative Production (Spanish initials UBPC) by subdividing large state agricultural enterprises into collectives working smaller units of land. Land was granted to the UBPCs in usufruct form under rent-free, open-ended leases. The means of production, previously property of the state enterprises, were sold to the UBPCs under soft credit terms.

In 2011, the new Economic and Social Guidelines of the Party and the Revolution stated that economic policy would correspond to the principle that only socialism is capable of overcoming difficulties and preserving the conquests of the revolution and that, in addition to the socialist state enterprises that would constitute the main form of the national economy, other forms of management would also be recognized and promoted. Cooperatives would form part of the new economic model, not only tied to agriculture but also in other sectors of the economy. The next year, the *Gaceta Extraordinaria* No. 53 published the norms to regulate the creation, operation, and dissolution of these new cooperatives, known as Non-Agricultural Cooperatives. These are cooperatives of workers devoted to production or services. Thus the Cuban cooperative movement ceased to be an exclusively agricultural phenomenon.

Non-Agricultural Cooperatives within the Updating of the Economic Model

Four years after their initial authorization, CNAs in Cuba remained an experiment, defined as "an organization with economic and social goals, voluntarily created by contribution of goods and rights and sustained by the work of its members, whose general objective is to produce goods and offer services through collective management to satisfy social needs and the needs of its members" (Decreto-Ley 305/2012).

CNAs are an additional employment option responding to the need to reduce the inflated employment rolls of the state sector, increase the supply of goods and services, and revive production and services that had disappeared in some parts of the country, such as sewing machine repair and the manufacture of items such as horseshoe nails and crematorium urns, among others.

Among the principles guiding the operations and functioning of CNAs, Decree-Law 305 lists: their voluntary nature; cooperation and mutual aid; collective decision-making and equal rights among members; autonomy and economic sustainability; cooperative internal discipline; social responsibility; contribution to planned development of the economy and the welfare of members and their families; and collaboration and cooperation between cooperatives and other entities. Formation of such an entity requires at least three founding members who must be Cuban residents, over eighteen years of age, and able to carry out the production or service work that is the cooperative's main activity.

These cooperatives may be first-level or second-level. The former are those created by the voluntary association of at least three persons, and the latter are those created by two or more first-level cooperatives. So far, no second-level cooperatives have been created, although the sixth section of the Special Dispositions of Decree-Law 305/2012 stated that within 360 days the Council of Ministers would issue regulations for this type of entity. The document called "Conceptualization of the Cuban Economic-Social Model of Socialist Development" was presented for discussion by the populace after the 2016 Seventh Congress of the Cuban Communist Party, and returned to this issue in its Guideline 167, but did not set a specific date for issuing regulations.

So far, therefore, the only CNAs are those of the first level, which can be formed with the criteria set forth in Decree-Law:

a. Through patrimony made up of the monetary contributions of "natural persons"[1] who voluntarily decide to associate among themselves under a system of collective property.

b. By natural persons who voluntarily decide to associate with the sole end of jointly acquiring inputs and services, commercializing products and services, or carrying out other economic activities, while the members retain ownership of their goods.

c. Through means of production that are state patrimony, such as buildings, which the state cedes for use under cooperative management through rent, usufruct grants, or other legal forms which do not imply a transfer of ownership.

d. A combination of the above three forms.

By the end of 2016, there were 498 approved CNAs, of which 23 percent were created under variant "a" and the remaining 77 percent under variant "c." No cooperative has yet been created through either of the other variants. Conversations with officials in charge of approving applications suggest that variants "b" and "d" are not taken into account.

Figure 5.1 shows the approval process for a CNA. If the proposal falls under variant "a," it is crafted and submitted by the founding members of the cooperative, after which the application follows the course shown in Figure 5.1. In the case of variant "c," the proposal can be prepared by the local body of People's Power (municipal or provincial government) or the national government body that wishes to see its enterprises or other budgeted units managed in cooperative form. In that case, the application is presented directly to the Permanent Commission for Implementation and Development, and the process then continues as in Figure 5.1. After approval of a state entity's changing its management model to a cooperative one, the workers are informed that they may become the future founding members of the newly approved cooperative. This is a long process with five levels of approval. The question arises: why aren't there more cooperatives given the desire to set them up, and does the fundamental problem lie in the number of steps, or in some other obstacle?

Figure 5.1: Approval Process for CNAs

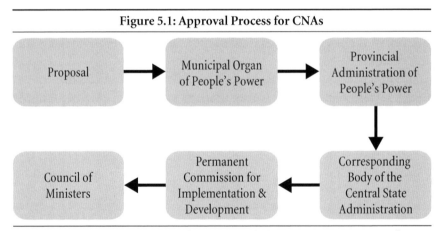

Source: Constructed by the author on the basis of Decree-Law 305 "De las Cooperativas No Agropecuarias," *Gaceta Oficial de la República de Cuba. Extraordinaria.* Number 53.

In a study carried out through workshops in the provinces of Pinar del Río, Havana, Artemisa, Villa Clara, Camagüey, and Holguín involving exchanges with cooperatives, cooperatives-in-formation, researchers, university professors, specialists from the National Association of Economists and Accountants of Cuba, and local officials, the following conclusions were reached.

The local government bodies of People's Power (that is, the municipal and provincial Administrative Councils) do not play a decisive role in the approval process. Rather, they forward to other entities the applications relating to cooperatives that would operate within their territories. Such cooperatives do generate greater numbers of businesses within the

territories, which in turn yield higher incomes, more jobs, and better living conditions for the community (Ojeda 2016, 77). These officials receive
many proposals to create new cooperatives, but some have been waiting
years to get approval from higher levels.

In the case of state enterprises that are being converted into cooperatives,
the Central State Administration entity involved may be a national ministry or a local or provincial government (depending on what state entity is
spinning off a state enterprise). This institution is considered to be the body
to which the cooperative would relate in the future (its órgano de relación),
and it is the one that proposes and supports its application for conversion.
It is also the institution that would be directly responsible for supervision,
evaluating the cooperative's operations and authorizing any merger, dissolution, division, or modification (Decreto-Ley 305/2012, 251). The decision to
give it a role in the decision to create a CNA assumes that it will know what
is best for the territory and for the cooperative; it is also given the power to
intervene in the autonomy of the newly created cooperative.

The next level of approval is by the Permanent Commission for Implementation and Development of the Guidelines, which in practice is the
Executive Group for Enterprise Improvement. This group is also in charge
of the whole fabric of enterprises in the country, so there is some question
as to its real capacity to analyze all the proposals it receives to establish
new cooperatives. A proposal includes: possible social objective, financial
design, real estate and other goods to be rented; goods or services that are
objects of state demand; prices of goods and services that are centrally
determined; environmental impact; and other aspects that must be evaluated in order to determine whether the proposal is viable or not.

Finally, the proposal reaches the Council of Ministers, which must approve
or reject businesses that would have a local impact and would contribute to
development. So far, the Council's criteria to decide on the approval or rejection of the creation of a new cooperative have not been made public.

The legislation governing the creation and functioning of the CNA does
not specify the branches of economic activity for which these new cooperatives may or may not be authorized. This has led the state to prioritize
their creation in sectors and entities in which state administration has not
been efficient. For proposals under variant "a," approval in the category of
meeting a social objective has depended on whether the idea is on the list
of activities already authorized for self-employment, which has the effect
of putting a brake on innovation.

The legislation has provided no stipulation of a time limit within which
proposals must be analyzed and forwarded, or not forwarded, to the next

level of the approval chain. The first group of cooperatives was approved in April 2013, the next in July of that same year and the third in October—that is, at a rate of a group every three months. The fourth group took a bit longer, five months, being approved in March 2014, and a fifth group has so far waited three years with no official word on when approvals might take place, which could signal another year's wait. Those who dream of creating a cooperative, meanwhile, live with the uncertainty of wondering what will happen in future meetings of the Council of Ministers.

Although the issue of setting response times emerges in all the events, seminars, workshops and exchanges about cooperatives, it has not been discussed at any of the sessions of the National Assembly of People's Power. It remains pending, with some cooperatives-in-formation that have been waiting three years for a response. This situation generates disincentives, uncertainty, and lack of confidence in the process.

Another aspect that generates lack of confidence and uncertainty is the possibility of the cooperative-to-be or its organizing committee negotiating with its corresponding state body (*organo de relación*) to determine the possible social objective, state demand for its product or service, and prices of goods and services that remain centrally set, among other aspects; in practice, such negotiation did not take place in almost any of the cooperatives visited by this author.

Decree 309/2012, in its fourth section, refers to participation in the process of soliciting bids for the state establishments or facilities whose realm of activity has been approved for cooperative management. This is further explained in Resolution 570/2012, articles 7–13, which indicates that the process should be transparent, with equal rights and opportunities for all participants, and that both the call for applications and the steps and requirements should be publicly announced in the mass media. However, this publicity has not been very effective because the cooperatives and cooperatives-to-be are unaware of the facilities that are being made available, or were at a given moment. The cooperatives that have participated in these conversions have learned of the opportunity through personal contacts, not through public announcements in any media.

According to data from the National Office of Statistics and Information (Spanish initials ONEI), at the end of January 2017 there were 397 functioning CNAs in existence, concentrated primarily in three activities: food services, retail sale of agricultural products, and construction, activities in which the Cuban state has historically been inefficient. Most of the CNAs are former state entities, which means that the new cooperative inherits the efficiency problems built up during the long years of state operation. Table 5.1 shows the distribution by areas of activity.

Table 5.1: CNAs in Operation, by Activity

Activity	Number
Retail sale of food, drink, and tobacco (farmers' markets)	103
Restaurants, coffee shops, and cafeterias	116
Construction	67
Hair salons and other beauty shops	22
Sale of birds	17
Recycling of non-metal garbage and wastes	15
Maintenance and repair of motor vehicles	8
Passenger transport	5
Accounting, auditing, and tax form preparation	6
Furniture making	5
Fabrication of metal products	4
Repair of personal effects and domestic appliances	4
Generation, storage, and distribution of electric energy	4
Garment manufacturing	5
Washing, dry cleaning and dyeing garments (textile and leather)	2
Processing of food and drinks	3
Manufacture of shoes, toys, and products of ceramics, plastic, glass, and marble	6
Manufacture of precision instruments	1
Manufacture of textile machinery	1
Fabrication of structural metal products	1
Printing	1
Wholesale sale of agricultural products	1
Total	**397**

Source: Constructed by the author from data from ONEI (January 2017).

In addition, the creation of these cooperatives has not been geographically spaced, for they are concentrated in Havana. Figure 5.2 shows this distribution more clearly. More than half of the total number of cooperatives in operation is located in Havana, followed somewhat distantly by the provinces of Artemisa and Matanzas. This raises the question, does the rest of the country want cooperatives as well? They do, but the approval process is long and some have been waiting years for a response.

Figure 5.2: Distribution of CNAs by Provinces

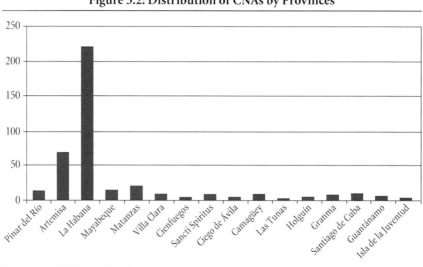

Source: Constructed by the author from data from ONEI (January 2017).

Despite the irregularities mentioned above, the experiment has had both economic and social successes that demonstrate the potential importance of cooperatives for the country and for improving its population's quality of life. The next section discussed the most important findings of the above-mentioned workshops, including information offered by the members of cooperatives-in-operation themselves. The section will also include data from the ninth national audit of the Comptroller General's Office[2] and the eighth legislative period of the National Assembly of People's Power.

Achievements in the Economic Sphere

In most cases, cooperative members' incomes have tripled within the first six months of operation. According to members' declarations, incomes in the form of monthly advances have varied around a median of about 2,500 CUP, without including the profits distributed at the end of the fiscal year; members say that, for the first time in years, they are living off the fruits of their labor.

According to data from the ninth national audit, the 291 CNAs reporting at the end of December 2014 declared 862.4 million pesos in revenue and 317.9 million in profits. At the end of November, 268 cooperatives had contributed CUP 87,727,000 in taxes, comprised of 51,780,000 in sales taxes, 33,506,000 in profit taxes, and 2,441,000 in payments for social security.

Plans are fulfilled because they are discussed and approved in the general assembly of the cooperative's members, which analyzes the true ability of the cooperative to meet the proposed goal. The state-originated cooperatives, when they were still state entities, did not fulfill their plans and operated with losses, a deficit that changed when they transformed their management model. Members say that now their planning takes into account the inputs that the cooperative has available to aid production, market conditions, and demand, among other factors; the plan is crafted collectively, which creates a commitment by the members. Members say that when they were state enterprises, the plan came from above in administrative fashion.

Members say that now they are concerned with lowering costs in a way that does not affect product or service quality, because if quality suffers, sales and income will suffer as well. Productivity and efficiency have grown without concentration of wealth. The cooperatives strive to be more efficient and productive every day, because of the resulting increase in the profits that are divided among all members at the end of the year.

The cooperative is concerned about the functioning of internal controls, which are voluntary, not imposed from above; members make sure that control and monitoring mechanisms are up to date. The means of production are better cared for, and the available material is used more efficiently. Acts of corruption and illegality have disappeared because now the members are the owners of the goods and the profits.

Achievements in the Social Sphere

Members of the cooperative feel like owners and attend to its proper operation. There is a commitment to meet the needs of the membership and to work to improve living conditions in the family and the larger social sphere. (In some cases, cooperatives have given interest-free loans to members facing difficulties.) The cooperative guarantees a more stable source of employment.

Democratic management prevails among the members: one member, one vote, participating in decision-making with equal rights. Members decide about economic issues and social life in the cooperative. The General Assembly determines, also democratically, whether a member should cease to be part of the cooperative; the decision is made on the basis of his or her performance as a member of this entity. Teamwork and collaboration generate optimism that stems from the shared decision-making power; all are equal: there are no bosses and no subordinates.

Cooperative members try to maintain and increase the quality of service or production because this translates to higher incomes and better living conditions for their families. Thus the majority of members is concerned with training and professional development, not only in accounting and economics but also in strategies for improving management and legal information to allow them to better defend their rights and be clear on what they can or cannot do. The cooperative is also able to search for alternative suppliers and customers; if one enterprise does not buy or sell from/to the cooperative, it can seek another one from a variety of different options (state enterprises, cooperatives, or private).

The cooperative develops ethical values such as mutual aid, responsibility, democracy, equality, equity, solidarity, transparency, collectivist sentiments, and environmental consciousness, and some cooperatives assist nursing homes, child care centers, and schools.

Problems Detected

Several problems have inhibited the potential best performance of the CNAs, however. This information was collected through the workshops and encounters mentioned above.

The process of creating cooperatives, as already noted, requires an excessive number of levels of approval, without deadlines for timely responses, which discourages such initiatives despite how necessary they are to solve local problems. The processes of approval of cooperatives and of conversion or rentals of state enterprises and properties to cooperatives are insufficiently transparent. In addition, information from banking institutions has been faulty regarding how to operate a CNA (about borrowing, authorized signatures, use of cooperative property, prerequisites for applying to the Trust Fund for new forms of non-state management, among other issues), a situation aggravated by the new members' lack of basic knowledge about a variety of banking services and how to access them.

In the case of cooperatives of state origin, the future founding members are given very little notice (from one week to fifteen days) of the impending change in the management model; consequently, their education about the transfer has been insufficient, centered only on legal and accounting matters. As a result, for too long (about a year, on average) cooperatives that have been spun off by the state sector fail to realize that they no longer have to wait for directions from higher authorities to define what they should or should not do. They are also slow to understand that they themselves must negotiate and make arrangements with their suppliers, customers, and markets. Out of ignorance of cooperative principles, some still allow state or government entities to interfere in their operations, limiting their autonomy.

At times, false cooperatives have been made up, of both state and private origin. Some continue to be state enterprises in fact yet operate under the name of cooperatives, while others take advantage of having "juridical personality"[3] to function as private businesses. In Cuba, private small or medium-sized enterprises have no legal standing, so cooperatives are utilized to fulfill this commercial purpose, in contradiction to the essence of what a cooperative should be.

Cooperatives only do basic accounting (bottom lines and general balances). They lack the capacity to carry out financial analyses, feasibility studies, or economic-financial projections. And, because the Cuban productive sector is weak, cooperatives cannot find necessary inputs in the domestic market; no efficient mechanisms have yet been established for importing needed materials, means of production, and technology. While cooperatives have access to state wholesale sellers within the country, these cannot supply 100 percent of the demand for products; they supply only between 30 percent to 50 percent,[4] which means that cooperatives must resort to the retail or clandestine markets, increasing the costs of their goods or services and generating dissatisfaction among the populace because of the resulting shortages in retail markets.

The state itself is somewhat suspicious of CNAs. On many occasions they are treated as if they were private businesses, or their juridical personality goes unrecognized, limiting their freedom of action. Moreover, the state agencies that do business with cooperatives are audited more frequently than others, with demands to justify their having contracted with a cooperative rather than another state agency. The internal control manuals given to the CNAs by the Comptroller General's Office are sixty-seven pages long, while those for state enterprises are only a third of that length, about twenty-one pages. Cooperatives and local government also fail to communicate sufficiently on how to work together to improve community conditions.

In more general terms, cooperative members lack knowledge of their duties and rights as cooperative members. They are inexperienced in writing contracts and seeing that they are fulfilled. Lack of proper training is a recurrent theme. There is chronic illiteracy regarding legislative, organizational, and management issues, which creates a vicious cycle that affects Cuban cooperative development. Cooperative members, future members, policy makers, regulators, officials, advisers, and all other actors are caught within this cycle, to greater or lesser degrees. This issue demands urgent attention, because the success of the desired process of transformation depends on good professional training.

In short, there is a contradiction between the formal political will to create cooperatives and building mechanisms for their successful operation. There is also no institution designed to group and represent the cooperatives. All of these problems obstruct the proper development of this new type of cooperative in Cuba. As a result, certain suggestions appear below toward the goal of contributing to improved performance.

Proposals to Improve Non-Agricultural Cooperative Performance

A coherent policy needs to be formulated to link the goal of creating CNAs to the regulatory framework and the behavior of all actors. A clear and consistent general law of cooperatives should be drafted. That law should reduce the number of steps required during the approval process. The levels at the Central State Administration, Permanent Commission, and Council of Ministers could be eliminated. Let new cooperatives be approved by municipal or provincial governments, which are best informed about the needs of their areas, and set response deadlines for confirming whether applications have been approved or not.

Make the process of offering state enterprise property to prospective cooperatives transparent and public as existing legislation requires, using the official communications media to inform the public about both requests for proposals and the results of applications. Create an effective procedure for changing a state management model to a cooperative one, in which:

- Cooperative principles are respected.
- Future members have the ability to negotiate the conditions of the change (social objective, rental price for buildings and other goods, what good and services will be demanded by the state and in what quantities, and other aspects that both sides judge to be pertinent).
- Courses on cooperative culture, legislation, accounting, and taxes are offered to future members.

Raise general knowledge of what a cooperative is and how it operates—among the populace, entities, decision-makers, regulators, and advisors. Create more educational spaces, open to cooperative members, on management and legal issues. Carry out feasibility studies. Facilitate processes of supply by, and contracting with, domestic enterprises. Include cooperatives in the national economic plan in order to eliminate distinctions between state and cooperative enterprises.

Allow the importation of materials that local sources cannot supply, or if the local materials lack the necessary quality or have non-competitive prices. Create means by which CNAs can export their products and services. This would improve quality, bring new flows of hard currency into the country, and guarantee the cooperatives the necessary hard currency to meet their own import needs.

Finally, improve communication with local governments to facilitate joint solutions to local problems, create an institution to support cooperative development (offering advice and support and aiding in the formation of new cooperatives), and facilitate communication with the state.

Conclusions

Non-Agricultural Cooperatives are a new model of management and property in Cuba that can bring important social benefits such as job creation, recovery of humanistic values, increased productivity and efficiency, import substitution, and improved quality of life for both cooperative members and the larger community. Therefore the experiment should continue to advance, with growth in the number of cooperatives in operation in the country and also with more transparency in the process.

The criteria to be applied in approving new cooperatives should be clear. Legislation should list the activities that are *not* considered priorities for development of cooperatives, leaving room for innovation and entrepreneurship in all other areas and thus promoting solutions of the many problems now troubling our domestic economy. Interrelations between the CNAs and state entities, banks, ministries, and local governments should be strengthened to enable the proper development of cooperatives and their contribution to the betterment of the community.

Finally, there is a need for new, non-experimental legislation to aid the progress of the cooperative movement in Cuba—a transparent law that offers needed incentives and relations with the rest of the economy, promoting an atmosphere of confidence, security, and clarity among cooperative members and the general populace.

Notes

1. A "natural person" (*persona natural*) is any individual who is able to acquire rights and contract obligations.
2. Full Spanish title, *Comprobación Nacional del Control Interno*. This is an annual audit, which in previous years had examined only state enterprises but has come to cover cooperatives as well.
3. "Juridical personality" (*personalidad jurídica*) is the ability to act as a legal subject, which is to say, the ability to acquire and possess all sorts of goods, to contract obligations and take legal actions, not as an individual but as an institution created by one or more physical persons to fulfill an objective, whether for profit or non-profit.
4. Information presented at the meeting held on 21 March 2015 in the Salón Central of the EXPOCUBA trade fair facility, where wholesale enterprises explained their services and how to access them to representatives of the new forms of non-state management.

Bibliography

Diario de Cuba. 2012. "Las cooperativas no agropecuarias podrán exportar e importar." Consulted at http://www.diariodecuba.com/cuba/14487-las -cooperativas-no-agropecuarias-podran-exportar-e-importar-pero-traves-de -empresas-esta, 9 April 2014.

Fernández Peiso, L. A. 2005. *El fenómeno cooperativo y el modelo jurídico nacional. Propuesta para la nueva base jurídica del cooperativismo en Cuba*. Doctoral thesis, University of Cienfuegos, 2005.

Hernández Morales, Aymara, and Carlos M. Arteaga Hernández, Eds. 2013. *Gestión integral cooperativa: guía para formadores y facilitadores*. Havana: MINAG.

Monzón, R. 2015. "Factores clave de éxito para lograr una gestión integral de las Unidades Básicas de Producción Cooperativa." In Beatriz Fortunata Díaz González, Ed., *Cooperativas y sociedad: un enfoque múltiple*. Havana: Editorial Universitaria.

Nova González, A. 2011. "Las cooperativas agropecuarias en Cuba: 1959–presente." In C. Piñeiro Harnecker, Ed., *Cooperativas y socialismo: Una mirada desde Cuba*, pp. 321–336. Havana: Editorial Caminos.

Ojeda Suris, D. 2014. *Un acercamiento a las cooperativas no agropecuarias de dos municipios de La Habana*. Havana: Centro de Estudios de la Economía Cubana.

———. 2015a. "Las cooperativas no agropecuarias como modelo de gestión de los servicios en Cuba, un análisis de su creación y funcionamiento." In *EKOTEMAS*, Volume I, Number 2.

———. 2015b. *Las Cooperativas no Agropecuarias: actualidad y perspectivas*. Havana: Centro de Estudios de la Economía Cubana.

———. 2016. "Las cooperativas no agropecuarias: dos años después." In J. García Ruiz, D. Figueras Matos, and E. González Mastrapa, Eds., *Sector cooperativo y desarrollo local: una visión desde las redes cubanas de investigación*, pp. 76–82. Villa Clara: Feijóo.

Rodríguez Delis, Livia. 2014. *Cooperativas no agropecuarias: de una experiencia a una novedad en Cuba.* In *Granma*, 30 April 2014.

Various authors. 2015. *Primer encuentro entre Cooperativas No Agropecuarias.* Havana, April 10, 2015.

6

New Actors and New Policies in Cuba: The Role of Credit Policy in the Reform

Jessica León Mundul and David J. Pajón Espina

Cuba's economic reforms undertaken during the 2010s, whose velocity is always announced as being gradual but persistent, seemed in 2015–2017 to be more unhurried than ever. Six years later, the economic slowdown in mid-decade could be attributed to collapse of the island's international relations and to exhaustion of the policy mechanisms implemented so far. Discussions at the 2016 Seventh Congress of the Cuban Communist Party essentially reaffirmed the previously announced course of action, the limits of the reform (most of them practically already reached), and extreme gradualness as a characteristic trait of economic policy decision-making.

The process of transformation was initially oriented toward economic efficiency and growth; the legitimizing discourse surrounding it later incorporated facets of social welfare and prosperity. Since its beginning in 2010, the reform has implied expansion and strategic diversification of a non-state sector linked to a state sector viewed, *a priori,* as the fundamental engine of economic growth.

In practice, while non-state forms have grown, particularly self-employment, *trabajo por cuenta propia* (TCP, after its Spanish acronym), their contribution to the country's growth and development have remained hostage to the design of an economic policy system that impedes fulfillment of their full potential and the generation of greater macro- and microeconomic benefits. The Seventh Congress and its documents (PCC 2016) did, for the first time, recognize the heterogeneity of the private sector and suggested the need to offer a defined legal status to certain undertakings, but they retained a subordinate role for the non-state sector and limits on the concentration of wealth and property.

In the general design of the reform, the sources of financing for the non-state sector were conceived on the basis of a new credit policy initiated in 2012. So far, its effects have been very limited. While the policy has undergone modifications, the dynamics of the non-state sector have remained fundamentally disconnected from the formal mechanisms that allocate financing.

We will assess the recent evolution of the regulatory framework of credit policy and its relation to the non-state sector (with emphasis on TCP) and reinforce the need for urgent changes, both in the design of credit policy and in the general conception of the reform. This step is essential to achieve a positive synergy between the mechanisms for allocating resources and the activation of a non-state sector that can generate a more dynamic development.

Evolution of the Regulatory Framework of Credit Policy

At the outset of the economic reform in 2010, the non-state sector faced serious financial restrictions ranging from lack of access to credit to the difficulty in opening and maintaining checking accounts or using other banking instruments (with the exception of the agricultural cooperatives).

In order to stimulate new forms of property and non-state management, the authorities sought to increase this sector's room for maneuver. To facilitate access to financing, a new credit policy went into effect in 2011 through Decree-Law 289 and Resolution 99 of the Banco Central de Cuba (BCC). Additional modifications were made when the range of possible non-state recipients of credit grew with the legalization of non-agricultural cooperatives (Spanish initials CNA) through Decree-Law 305 of 2012 and Instruction 5 of the BCC in 2013.

The November 2011 Decree-Law 289 established the principles and general procedures regulating credit and new banking services for individuals. It named new possible recipients of credit: authorized self-employed workers, small farmers with legal title to land, and other forms of non-state management to be authorized in the future, as well as individuals who needed to rebuild their houses or consume other material goods; in the last category, financing has been authorized only for purchase of cooking equipment (BCC 2014).

The institutions authorized to carry out this process were three state banks: the Banco Metropolitano (BM), Banco de Crédito y Comercio (BANDEC), and Banco Popular de Ahorro (BPA). These institutions also broadened their capacity to offer a number of banking services such as checking accounts in Cuban pesos (CUP) or convertible pesos (CUC), thus favoring the use of payment instruments such as letters of exchange, checks, and others. Neither this initial regulatory framework nor later updatings of the policy have made room for non-state or foreign agents to assume roles as issuers of credit.

Initially, the regulatory framework of the credit policy did not distinguish among potential beneficiaries and posed numerous practical barriers to access to credit.[1] The regulations stipulated credits only in CUP, with a minimum of 3,000 CUP for terms of eighteen months or less for working capital and five years for investment. Interest payments were based essentially on the rates established for deposits, plus a margin ranging from 0.5 percent to 2.5 percent. For credits involving 60 months, the rates were directly established by the BCC (see Table 6.1).

Table 6.1: Interest Rates for Working Capital and Investment		
Months	Minimum	Maximum
3	2.50	3.50
6	3.00	4.00
12	4.50	5.50
24	5.50	7.50
36	6.50	8.50
60	7.00	9.00
72	7.50	9.50
84	7.60	9.60
96	7.70	9.70
108	7.85	9.85
120	8.00	10.00

Source: Constructed by the authors based on BCC, 2012.

The issuance of credit only in CUP is consistent with the goal of re-establishing that currency's central function, as part of an ongoing process of currency unification. Implicitly, it assumes that the demand for convertible pesos or foreign hard currencies can be satisfied through individuals authorized to carry out self-employment making use of the CADECA exchange market.

The regulatory framework also required various documents that would testify to the existence and operation of a formal business and to its actual and projected economic results. In terms of guarantees and collateral, borrowers could present co-signers with demonstrable ability to pay; bank accounts in the credit-issuing bank; and certificates of deposit in some of the commercial banks, among other possibilities. The aim was to cover repayment of both principal and interest in case of delays in loan repayment. As can be seen in Peña (2012) and Banco Metropolitano (2012), this regulatory framework sought to achieve 100 percent coverage of the risk of non-payment.

In general, the initial policy failed to recognize the specific internal dynamics of the complex non-state sector, and its barriers to credit access drove away an important set of potential borrowers. By December 2012, a year after implementation, only 0.1 percent of the total sum of credit issued under the new policy had gone to TCPs (Martínez 2015). In view of the meager financing directed to the non-state sector, the credit policy has since been revised on several occasions in search of more flexible legal framework and greater access to credit. Among the main modifications have been the following:

- More flexibility regarding the minimum amounts of loans that could be requested before a loan could be granted as well as the length of the repayment periods, lowering the former to 1,000 CUP and increasing the latter to ten years for investments, and establishing the possibility of lower floors and longer repayment times in exceptional situations. In the case of small farmers, the floor is only 500 Cuban pesos, and there is no ceiling for maximum total loans.
- Broadening the loan guarantees to include jewels, patrimonial goods, and agricultural goods, among others. The task of assessing the value of these goods was assigned to specific state institutions such as the División Coral Negro of the state corporation CIMEX for jewelry, and the Registro Nacional de Bienes Culturales de la República de Cuba for goods considered national patrimony. Demands for collateral have been gradually loosened, with the level of risk coverage reduced as a matter of policy to 60 percent (Cubadebate 2015b).
- Expanding the capacity of banking personnel and creating specialized departments for credit issuance in particular bank networks: the BPA created a department to promote financial services and products, the BM created an Office of Credit, and the BANDEC created the position of micro-credit officer with the possibility of making visits to the sites of non-state businesses.[2]
- Increasing hours of public access to bank branches.
- Recognizing the diversity of agents making up the non-state sector. Setting criteria of selection for the promotion of particular forms of property and management and particular sectors of interest, including policy actions such as:
  - Allowing CNAs that had remained ineligible as borrowers, according to the credit policy requirements, to access a trust fund with

resources from the state budget. Such a fund would also cover 100 percent of the risks associated with initial capital loans and 75 percent of those related to working capital and investment for a term of two years, as well as acting as co-signer.[3]

- Applying lower interest rates to working capital credits and to investment loans for agricultural activities of interest to the government, with the state budget absorbing part of the cost (Cubadebate 2016).
- Understanding the need to create more favorable conditions of credit access for TCPs just beginning their activity, that is, start-ups (Martínez 2015). However, the regulatory institutions have not spelled out the specific actions to be taken in favor of this segment.

The legal framework of credit policy ratified the role of the non-state sector in the new economic model, and it contributed somewhat to facilitate its access to financial services and credits in comparison to that of Cuban state enterprises. In addition, the incorporation of the CNAs required the introduction of differentiated treatment. Nonetheless, what has been legislated and put into practice by banking institutions has maintained a basically homogeneous treatment, particularly among TCPs.

Results of the Implementation of the Credit Policy: Limits and Potentials

In October 2010, the government authorized the first group of activities that could be carried out by private producers. That measure was rolled out along with others that encouraged the shift of a considerable number of workers to the legal non-state sector: these included the new possibility to hire workers and the announcement and later implementation of "labor availability" (reducing the number of excess workers in the state sector). By December 2011, the number of self-employed workers had grown to more than 200,000, even though they still lacked access to wholesale markets and formal sources of financing and were operating in isolation and disadvantage with regard to the state sector.

Available periodic figures on the number of credits that have been granted allow for an estimate of the share directed toward a broad grouping made up of TCPs, CNAs, small farmers, and individuals buying cooking equipment. Although the total going exclusively to the TCPs is unknown, it can be assumed to be lower, given the limited quantities previously destined to this group. The evolution over time of the number of self-employed and of the awarding of credit, which began in December 2011, is reflected in Figure

6.1. The two processes are seen to be disconnected: the rates of expansion and exhaustion in the non-state sector have depended on engines of growth other than the state's policy on credit availability.

Figure 6.1: Evolution of Self-Employment (TCP) and Cumulative Number of Credits Issued to TCPs and Other Non-State Sector Entities*

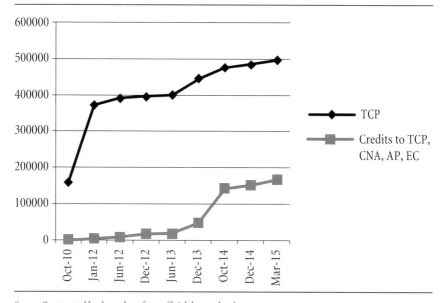

Source: Constructed by the authors from official data and estimates.
*TCP = self-employment; CNA = nonfarm cooperatives; AP = Small farmers; EC = consumer loans (limited to purchase of cooking equipment).

A year and a few months after the opening to self-employment, this authorization had contributed to the formalization of activities that a significant number of people had been carrying out illegally, and the occupation of production niches that had not been permitted until then. This sector functioned even though there were no bank credits, or where such credits were seldom issued even after the practice had been authorized. By the end of 2013, with 444,109 self-employed, only 550 credits had been issued to this group (EFE 2013). In general, most credits applied for within the framework of the new policy have been used for financing the purchase of construction materials and building projects in individual homes.

After 2014, the number of credits granted grew significantly compared to earlier periods, responding somewhat to the changes in the regulatory framework and banking practice. Although this may seem to suggest a contribution to the rate of growth of TCP, in practice any such contribution was marginal, as an analysis of the composition of the credits granted shows:

- Small farmers accounted for almost 95 percent of the loans (Martínez 2014) represented in Figure 6.1.
- Since January 2014, the statistic has included credits for cooking equipment.
- There have been several waves of approvals of CNAs since July 2013. By January 2014, 73 percent of CNAs had requested credit (Piñeiro 2014), a proportion that may well remain stable or even grow given the advantages conferred on CNAs by the trust fund.

Also notable is the slowdown in growth of TCP as compared to earlier periods. The initial rate of growth was about 135 percent from October 2010 to January 2013. After the initial surge followed by more moderate but sustained growth, early 2016 saw the first drop in the number of people employed in this sector, to 496,400 (Peña R. F., 2016), less than the half million reported in 2015.

As for total credits granted to TCPs, these grew notably in 2014 in comparison to earlier periods (more than 31 million CUP, ten times greater than 2013, see Figure 6.2). Despite this increase, the average loan has been about 780 CUC, a strikingly insufficient amount if the goal is to expand any productive capacity, given the level of input prices (León 2015) and means of production.

Figure 6.2: Total Annual Credits Issued to TCPs (in Thousands of CUP)

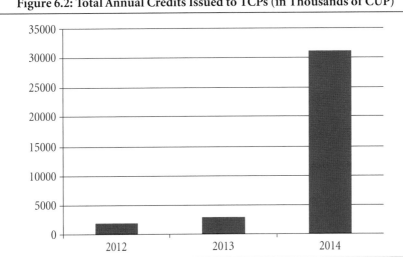

Source: Constructed by the authors based on Martínez N. 2015.

The extent of these credits offered by specific banks also show a disconnect between the dynamism of new non-state forms and the provision of financing for them. As of December 2014, the Banco Metropolitano—which operates only in the capital city, home to the highest proportion of TCPs, 27 percent of the total—had issued only 6 percent of total credits (see Table 6.2). This same bank holds 34 percent of checking accounts opened by the self-employed and non-farm cooperative members. The discrepancy suggests, alarmingly, that these depositors see the importance of banking services but make use of only a portion of them.

Table 6.2: Structure of Checking Accounts and of Credits Issued by Banks* for the Self-Employed (TCP) and CNA (Nonfarm Cooperatives)

Bank	Bank accounts opened, TCP and CNA (as % of total)	Credits issued, TCP and CNA (as % of total)
BPA	18.7	49.2
BANDEC	47.3	44.8
BM	34.0	6.0

Source: Martínez N. 2015.

*BPA: Banco Popular de Ahorro; BANDEC: Banco de Crédito y Comercio; BM: Banco Metropolitano.

The disconnect between credit issuance and the new non-state forms, especially TCP, stems from the fact that credit policy, as it was initially conceived, has not been attractive to private actors and new entrepreneurs. Later modifications have been insufficient to alter this picture. In 2014, funds immobilized in banks, as family savings accounts, represented approximately 27 percent of gross domestic product (GDP) (ONEI 2015), yet at the end of 2015, the total credits issued to the population by the BPA amounted to a bit less than 28 percent of that sector's savings (Borrás 2016). Thus, it appears that restricted access to credit is due to barriers created by the design of the policy, not to a lack of financial resources.

While it is true that the circulation of this portion of the money supply, currently immobilized in commercial banks, could generate pressures on currency stability via inflation of the Cuban peso and instability in CADECA exchange rates, the proper allocation of these financial resources to activities that could generate higher levels of production and services (particularly in the marketable sector) is essential to strengthen the economic contribution of the new forms of production. Such a measure is not destabilizing if it succeeds in truly stimulating economic activity.

The credit policy's self-definition reduces the range of possible borrowers because it establishes that a beneficiary must already have a business in formal operation with a degree of consolidation that allows for retrospective oversight and future projections. Thus, anyone seeking to start a project, or even anyone with a project newly under way, remains outside the framework of this financing mechanism. The remaining options are to seek other sources of semi-legal or illegal financing or simply to give up on a project that may have helped to escape poverty or irregularity.

This policy design not only explicitly favors already existing agents, but it also creates barriers to the entry and development of new competitors in the non-state sector. Thus, the prohibitions that for years created collusive behavior in various sectors are in effect continuing. Such an atmosphere of restricting competition leads to the proliferation of major predatory practices that seek maximum profits through the frequent exercise of market power to the detriment of both consumers and new providers. While banking sector authorities seem to have perceived the vulnerability of potential entrepreneurs or recently started businesses in their access to financing, they have not undertaken concrete actions to guarantee greater inclusion.

This discriminatory strategy is not limited to distinctions within the TCP sector. Within the larger non-state sector, non-farm cooperatives have, as noted above, been granted the possibility of access to a trust fund, which the available evidence suggests they have been utilizing. Because cooperatives, in theory, generate production dynamics of a more social character, policy makers *a priori* have given them an advantaged position.

Still, this privileged access to the trust fund seems to include projects that are not necessarily better than those growing out of variants of TCP. The majority of approved cooperative projects have involved the transfer of state functions (sometimes shed by the state because of their inefficiency) rather than true initiatives of a spontaneous or entrepreneurial character. As of May 2014, 77 percent of the approved cooperatives were of state origin (Piñeiro 2014). One positive element, however, is that this regulation does establish a precedent for differentiated policies based on establishing selection criteria.

Meanwhile, various aspects related to the guarantees demanded of borrowers continue to constitute disincentives for beginning the process of requesting a loan. Although the range of possible guarantees has been broadened and specific banking practices have relaxed the goal of covering 100 percent of the risk, they still fall short. For example, sharing the risks inherent to entrepreneurship, such as the state support (trust fund) for CNAs, have not been extended to other non-state forms.

Methods to assess the value of goods offered as collateral create additional disincentives and barriers. In the case of jewels and gems, applicants must come personally to Havana no matter where they live; for automobiles to be used as collateral, they must have been manufactured after 1974

(Cuba Contemporánea 2014). This means that the many owners of older cars will find it impossible to use them as guarantees. This regulation completely ignores the high market value of, for instance, U.S.-built pre-1959 cars, which are sought after either to restore them to mint condition or because their technical characteristics make them highly profitable.

Strengthening the impact of credit policy depends on better allocation of financial resources by considering such aspects as: export capacity, technologically complex production processes, contribution to import substitution, job creation, use of skilled labor, contribution to local and regional development, and closing gaps in equity and offering more room for the entry of new competitors.

For decision-makers, one of the most important challenges is to understand the potential of a credit policy that considers social and national gains beyond the profitability of the commercial bank. This requires both the identification of such selection criteria (not necessarily at odds with bank operating margins) and national and local state budgeting that is more inclined to support non-state endeavors by sharing their risks.

The lending institutions also have features that lessen the effectiveness of the credit policy. The limited number of institutions, the *a priori* segmentation of the market permitted for the operation of each institution, and the existence of a sole owner (the Cuban state) limit the benefits of competition and the impetus of innovations to attract new clients. Likewise, instead of providing individual incentives linked to owners' profits and employees' stimulus, which in private foreign banks can spur the creation of new financial products and broaden the range of clients, Cuba and its state banks offer perverse incentives: more work in a context of mostly inflexible salaries.

Analyzing the modifications both in the legal framework and in banking practice leads us to infer that the authorities have been conscious of the limitations of the policy as measured by the number and size of credits oriented toward the non-state sector and also that they have tried to reverse this situation. However, other factors related to the inconsistency of policies in the context of the economic reform have outweighed such efforts, perpetuating the disconnect between formal financial mechanisms and the private sector.

In the first place, the required scrutiny of potential clients keeps a significant number of the self-employed away from the banks. In general, the self-employed operate in asymmetrical conditions with respect to the state sector (with which they establish only limited contractual relations) and remain cut off from access to wholesale markets and formal channels for importation, which means that they carry out a considerable number of operations outside the legal realm. A self-employed businessperson in such conditions will have inconsistent cash flows that will not stand up to any analysis that considers only the accounting of its strictly legal operations.

Second, high levels of under-declared incomes create a contradiction: for borrowers to demonstrate their ability to repay sizable loans, they would have to present projections that imply large sales volume and, thus, later increases in tax bills. Recall that all the banks involved in this process are state owned. In 2014, only seven percent of taxpayers filing formal returns declared balances of income and expenses that called for taxes on personal income, and levels of under-declaring were detected in sixty percent of those audited (Cubadebate 2015a), for a total of 130 million pesos (Sosín 2014). For 2015, 68,000 persons were found to have under-declared their net revenues (Castro 2016), a high figure although 10 percent lower than the previous year.

Considering all the facets of the big picture, existing businesses of significant scope and with good prospects for success, but lacking sufficient endogenous resources, will look for financing via informal means, that is, semi-legal or illegal sources. Therefore, the context creates pressure for the best projects to remain outside the purview of the official policy.

Moreover, the marginal character of many of the approximately two hundred occupations authorized for self-employment limits the quality of projects that might require financing. Perhaps it may not precisely influence the entrepreneurs' need for resources (any *cuentapropista* may need these regardless of the complexity of his or her activity), but it affects the quality of the production they generate, and thus their potential contribution to the country's growth and development. Even in the cooperative sphere, official declarations have projected a vision of marginality, by stating that such forms of production ". . . do not play significant roles in the country's economic development and whose state management has, so far, been ineffective" (Puig & Martínez 2013).

Thus the initial expansion of self-employment before the opening of the credit market, followed by implementation of a policy that is exclusive rather than inclusive and is immersed in a context inhospitable to fulfilling the potential of the non-state sector, has pushed the demand for loans toward alternative sources. One may be funds accumulated through legal or illegal means by individuals who took advantage of privileged positions during the era before the current reform (positions they still occupy, in many cases). The most significant share of informal sources came from outside the country, entering in the form of remittances or clandestine investment.

The sum total of remittances entering the country has been variously estimated at between $1.2 and $3 billion a year (Spadoni 2015), without counting those sent in kind. Rodríguez (2015) reports that ". . . about 50 percent of remittances function as working capital or investment for the private or cooperative sector." Given a domestic market characterized by irregular supply and deficient quality and variety, a notable contribution to the development of the new businesses is the importation of personal goods that end up as means of production or working capital. This import channel becomes an effective response to the exclusion of the non-state sector from participating in the formal mechanisms of foreign commerce.

However, the option of resorting to external financing or other sources of accumulation is not available to every Cuban. A negative facet of the reform has been the concentration of benefits in the hands of privileged social groups, those possessing tangible and intangible resources that put them in a position to skillfully take advantage of stimuli and choose among various options to create or expand their activity, while poor Cubans "who cannot count on family remittances and who do not have social or political capital will remain excluded from the benefits of the reform" (Hansing and Optenhögel 2015, 12).

In light of this division, credit policy offers little support for vulnerable groups. In terms of employment, 596,500 jobs were cut from the state sector payroll between 2009 and 2014 (Cuban Contemporánea 2014). Those workers, the majority of whom were among the losers in the truncated reform of the '90s (their salaries in the public sector are meager, and their jobs the most expendable), generally lack the resources to mount a successful business; if they are absorbed by the private sector, it is most likely as hired employees. This situation has worrisome implications for state workers, hemmed in by future reductions in workforce, the limits on non-state sector growth, and the initial expansion of self-employment that involved a considerable number of persons without previous formal work ties.

Conclusion

In this chapter, we have combined analyses of the regulatory framework, specific bank practices, the burden of an economic order insufficiently transformed to accompany the reforms under way, and the post-2010 patterns in the non-state sector. Our examination has revealed a credit policy that is highly homogeneous and unable to unleash the potential of productive forces. That inability stems from technical aspects of the policy's design but also from economic policy inconsistencies that are broader than the technical details of the credit-issuance mechanisms.

Among the aspects that place barriers between formal financing mechanisms and the actions of non-state firms, the most striking are: the absence of competition in the commercial banking sector; the limited list of authorized non-state activities (meager in size and practically nineteenth-century in description); high levels of tax evasion, conditioned by *cuentapropistas'* very limited room for maneuver that causes them to avoid scrutiny of their accounts; and, in general, a design for the non-state sector that views it as being outside the dynamics that can generate a serious contribution to development.

In spite of the ever more pressing need for changes, the path laid out by the Seventh Congress of the Cuban Communist Party in April 2016 reaffirmed a subordinate role for the non-state sector and extended a blanket of doubt over the treatment of riches that result from entrepreneurial success. Meanwhile, the idea that the banking and financial sector should capture and channel savings toward prioritized sectors and productive development, and should provide access to financial services, is also represented in the Party documents. This appears to be one more of the many contradictions emanating from the current reform.

In sum, today's credit policy contributes to the exclusion of the sectors least favored by the current and past reforms. Through its support of the most empowered, it accentuates equity gaps. It also continues to immobilize resources that could be allocated to support new undertakings; when it does offer them, it ignores a potential group of beneficiaries and is incapable of recognizing the contribution to the country's growth and development that authorized activities could make.

Even in a continued general context that does not completely favor these productive forces and a full development of the intrinsic potential of issuing credit, it is possible to align credit policy with the interests of the non-state sector. To do this it would be important for the authorities to consider international experiences, with special attention to the realm of microfinance. Despite the heterogeneity of Cuba's non-state sector, the predominance of small and medium-sized enterprises suggests the advantages of expanding a segment of the banking and financial sector to focus on those enterprises' needs.

It will also be necessary to consider eliminating restrictions on new and fledgling enterprises, equalize the access of various forms of property to financing mechanisms, recognize the heterogeneity of the non-state sector, establish selection criteria designed from a pro-development perspective, and give the state a more active role in sharing the risks that development of promising projects entails.

Notes

1. For more on specifics of the regulatory framework, see León and Pajón, 2013 and 2015.
2. See AIN 2015 and Rosabal 2015.
3. See AIN 2015 and Rosabal 2015.

Bibliography

AIN. 2015. "Banco de Crédito y Comercio financia a trabajadores por cuenta propia." In *Granma*. 16 June, p. 2.

Banco Metropolitano. 2012. Instrucción Transitoria No. 237.

Banco Central de Cuba (BCC). 2011. Circular No.1/2011.

———. 2012. Circular No. 2/2012.

———. 2013. Instrucción No. 5/2013.

———. 2013. Instrucción No. 88/2013.

———. 2014. Instrucción No. 1/2014.

Borrás, F. 2016. "Papel de los bancos comerciales en la promoción de la inclusión financiera: avances de investigación." Paper presented at Seminario Anual, Center for the Study of the Cuban Economy, Havana, March.

Castro, Y. 2016. "Pagar bien y en tiempo." In *Granma*. 8 January, p. 2.

Cuba Contemporánea. 2014. "Más de cien mil cubanos contratados en negocios del sector no estatal." 8 October.

Cubadebate. 2015a. "El pago de los tributos: la disciplina que falta." In *Cubadebate*, 15 January.

———. 2015b. "Crece el número de préstamos otorgados para reparar viviendas." In *Cubadebate*, 22 April.

———. 2016. "Cuentas claras sobre el Presupuesto del Estado." In *Cubadebate*. 18 February.

Echevarría, D. 2015. "Equidad y desarrollo en Cuba: oportunidades y retos." Paper presented at the Taller de Investigación, CEEC-Universidad de Pinar del Río. Pinar del Río, 18 February.

EFE. 2013. "Créditos para incentivar sector privado no han tenido el efecto deseado." In *Panorama Mundial*. Number 252, 30 December.

Espina, M. P. 2012. "Retos y cambios en la política social." In P. Vidal and O. E. Pérez, Eds., *Miradas a la economía cubana: el proceso de actualización*. Havana: Editorial Caminos.

Hansing, K., and U. Optenhögel. 2015. "Cuba: las desigualdades se tornan visibles. Consecuencias de la economía de escasez y reforma." In *Nueva Sociedad*. Number 255, January–February.

León, J. 2015. "Marco de consistencia para el análisis y evaluación de la estabilidad monetaria en la economía cubana." Master's thesis, Universidad de La Habana.

León, J., and D.J. Pajón. 2013. "Emprendimientos y política crediticia en el modelo económico cubano." In O. E. Pérez and R. Torres, Eds., *Cuba: la ruta necesaria del cambio económico*. Havana: Editorial Ciencias Sociales.

————. 2015. "Política crediticia en Cuba: evolución reciente y efectos sobre el sector no estatal." In O. Pérez and R. Torres, *Miradas a la economía cubana. Análisis del sector no estatal*, pp. 105–113. Havana: Editorial Caminos.

Martínez, L. 2014. "Economía cubana avizora mayores crecimientos en el 2015." In *Granma*. 30 November.

Martínez, N. 2015. "La nueva política bancaria: Una valoración de los créditos para los trabajadores por cuenta propia." Diploma paper, X Diplomado de Administración Pública, Banco Central de Cuba.

Ministerio de Justicia. 2010. *Gaceta Oficial de la República de Cuba,* Number 012 Ext. Especial, 8 October.

————. 2011. *Gaceta Oficial de la República de Cuba,* Number 40 Extraordinaria.

————. 2012. *Gaceta Oficial de la República de Cuba*, Number 053 Extraordinaria, 11 December.

————. 2013a. *Gaceta Oficial de la República de Cuba*, Number 027, 26 September.

————. 2013b. *Gaceta Oficial de la República de Cuba*, Number 004 Extraordinaria, 21 February.

ONEI. 2014. *Anuario Estadístico de Cuba 2013*. Havana: ONEI.

————. 2015. *Anuario Estadístico de Cuba 2014.* Havana: ONEI.

PCC. 2016. *Conceptualización del modelo económico y social cubano de desarrollo socialista/Plan nacional de desarrollo económico y social hasta 2030: propuesta de visión de la nación, ejes y sectores estratégicos.* Havana: Seventh Congress of the Cuban Communist Party.

Peña, H. 2012. "Política crediticia interna cubana. Antecedentes y situación actual." In *Revista del Banco Central de Cuba*. Number 3:3.

Peña, R. F. 2016. "Micro, pequeña y mediana empresa en Cuba: ¿son empresarios los cuentapropistas?" In *On Cuba*, 26 January.

Piñeiro, C. 2014. "Cooperativas no agropecuarias en La Habana. Diagnóstico preliminar." In various authors, *Economía cubana: transformaciones y desafíos*, pp. 291–334. Havana: Ciencias Sociales.

Puig, Y., and L. Martínez. 2013. "Cooperativas no agropecuarias. Una apuesta por la eficiencia." In *Granma*. 5 July.

Rodríguez, J. L. 2015. "Cuba: desempeño económico en 2014 y proyecciones para 2015 (I)." In *Cubadebate*, 7 January.

Rosabal, H. 2015. "Banca en Cuba: Créditos sin demanda." In *Bohemia*, 7 January.

Sosín, E. 2014. "Impuestos no tan impuestos." In *OnCuba*, 19 February.

Spadoni, P. 2015. "Descongelamiento de las relaciones entre los Estados Unidos y Cuba: impacto potencial en la economía cubana." In R. Torres, O. E. Pérez, F. Castellacci, and C. Brundenius, Eds., *Cuba en un nuevo escenario. Perspectivas de desarrollo económico*, pp. 49–66. Havana: Publicaciones Acuario.

Triana, J. P., and J. León. 2014. "Hacia la unidad cambiaria y monetaria." In Cuba Study Group, *Desde la Isla*. Number 23.

7

Innovation in Cuban State Enterprises: Limitations

Ileana Díaz Fernández, Humberto Blanco Rosales, and Orlando Gutiérrez Castillo

Introduction

In April 2016, the Seventh Congress of the Cuban Communist Party approved a resolution on the results of the implementation of the Guidelines of Economic and Social Policy. It stressed "the continuity of the process begun five years ago" (PCC 2016b), consistent with the vision of a "sovereign, independent, socialist, prosperous, and sustainable" nation (PCC 2016c), affirmed by the resolution on the 2030 National Economic and Social Development Plan.

In today's world, a country's sustainable development, its place in the international arena, and its inhabitants' prosperity require effective national systems for innovation. For the stimulus to be effective, economic enterprises, which are the entities that create wealth, must enjoy all the internal conditions needed to generate innovations, and the institutional environment in which they act must favor the necessary supports, interactions, and incentives. This chapter seeks to show the problems and obstacles that face Cuban state enterprises seeking to innovate. The central point will be the need for fewer regulations and more innovation-promoting incentives.

This study makes use of the results of past studies by Blanco (2013), Blanco and Gutiérrez (2014), Díaz (2012, 2013, 2014), Gutiérrez (2013), Cazull, Hernández, and Sánchez (2012), García and Hernández (2010), and Marcelo (2011), all of which assess microeconomic factors of innovation in Cuban state enterprises; these include structure, authority, strategy, and innovation management, as observed in a selected group of such enterprises.

The chapter is organized as follows: first, conceptual issues regarding the topic of innovation; second, an analysis of the regulatory framework as it relates to innovation; third, the results of an innovation management diagnostic in Cuban state enterprises; and a concluding section.

Some Conceptual Issues

We start with the assumption that development is endogenous, in accordance with specific conditions of space and time. It would be a socially shared project and strategy. It involves a necessary and coherent combination of market and state mechanisms to lead toward the solution of innumerable problems in economy and society (Alonso and Triana 2013). Development requires the participation of various economic agents (representing different forms of property) in a transparent institutional context that facilitates and regulates their interactions.

If we agree that scientific and technological progress is very important to endogenous growth, then a point made by Guzmán (2006, 365) must also be borne in mind: "The entrepreneur's role in the implementation of new technology in the productive mechanism is not made explicit. Rather, there is an abstracted entrepreneurial factor, which may or may not really exist, because not all economies or all countries have an available or potential enterprise structure with sufficient capacity to take on and put into practice the productive processes that can emerge from new technological advances."

No society has achieved high levels of economic and social development without adequately promoting innovation and knowledge accumulation. Those processes take place in enterprises; they may resolve the challenges to meet societies' material and spiritual needs.

The most frequently used definition of innovation was put forward in the Oslo Manual (2005), on which we rely in this chapter: "An innovation is the introduction of a new or significantly improved product (good or service) or process, a new marketing method, or a new organizational method in business practices, workplace organization, or external relations" (OECD 2005b, 56). This definition may be criticized for lacking a social approach, but for our purposes that issue may be set aside.

According to the Bogotá Manual, however, developing countries are less concerned with developing radical innovations and more oriented to learning processes. Therefore the goal of measuring innovation should be to "identify firms that are actively involved in technological change and are making promising achievements in 'Innovative Activity Management,' regardless of their results (or 'objective innovations'), and also to identify the main hurdles that innovative processes have to confront in the region" (RICYT 2001, 57). This chapter will concentrate on those issues within Cuban state firms.

Innovation is not a linear process and involves risks. It tends to move in two patterns related to Schumpeter's notion of creative accumulation and creative destruction. The first is present in routinized structures in large firms, with a pattern of research + development + innovation (Spanish initials I+D+i); the second involves a more entrepreneurial logic that, as a rule, generates new businesses that may emerge out of large firms. The processes of creative destruction may lead to the closure of inefficient firms and their replacement by others whose performance is efficient and innovative.

Viewed from an organizational perspective, innovation is a key internal process through which—in accordance with contextual requirements, conditions, objectives and strategies—an organization assimilates, generates, and puts into practice ideas that lead it to introduce new products, services, processes, and management approaches, all of which enrich the organization's value to the customers whose needs and demands must be satisfied.

Innovation is closely related to how the organization is managed. Following the idea that "every technological revolution brings about a change in common sense" (Pérez 2000, 4), the change in common sense in the management realm has to do with a change in administrative approaches that are indispensable to achieve sustained levels of growth and effectiveness based on, among other factors, innovation.

To foster innovation the enterprise builds a culture that involves workers in knowledge-generation and decision-making in order to strive for continuous improvement through incremental innovations; among others, to meet customer needs with more flexible and horizontal organizational structures. This approach also must be part of a strategic management perspective that takes the organization's central competencies into account and considers how to improve them or create others to interact with the environment in the most effective way.

Thus, innovation management favors conducting and coordinating the available resources to increase new knowledge and generate ideas that allow for new or improved products, services, and processes. This implies developing a set of functions including vigilance, enrichment, evaluation, optimization, and protection. The first refers to being alert to new technological trends and the strategies of competitors, and identifying potential sources of opportunity for innovation. Enrichment establishes the profiles of competitiveness and of its own differentiated potential in order to define possible strategic directions. Evaluation identifies the potentials for increasing the enterprise's resources by investing in human capabilities and technology (whether internal, external, or mixed via cementing of strategic alliances). Optimization means employing resources in the best way to achieve efficiency. Protection safeguards internal innovations and engages in continual updating of the enterprise's knowledge.

Therefore increasing the effectiveness of innovation management is not simply a synonym for high I+D+i budgets. Rather, it means generating intense processes of innovation through the development and consolidation of appropriate environments within the firm (Hamel and Prahalad 1999). In that sense, effective innovation management demands enterprise autonomy as well as incentives from the wider organizational context to stimulate the development of innovations.

State Enterprises: Analysis of the Current Regulatory Framework

A historical review of the Cuban state enterprise system from 1959 to today reveals that it has passed through several different phases displaying the following regularities:

- Over time, enterprises have utilized different management systems with various degrees of uniformity and centralization, and different forms of internal organization. However, over time the process of enterprise creation and organization has generated excessive uniformity, with a predominance of large units.
- The underlying dilemma in Cuban state enterprises has been to prescribe what degree of decision-making capacity is granted to them and how much autonomy their management teams should have in order to lead them effectively. The prevailing tendency has clearly been one of excessive centralization, highly complex and rigid organizational structures, and little enterprise autonomy.
- The central axis on which management and administration rest has been the annual plan. It is crafted according to mandatory indicators that enterprises receive from higher levels (most often, from the Ministry of Economics and Planning), accompanied by limited allocations of financial and material resources (including energy). This notably reduces their room for maneuver, ability to adapt to changing conditions, and future development because of both the operative nature of the planning process and the excess of mandatory indicators.
- In the realm of innovation, the predominant tendency has been toward incremental innovations to solve particular production problems pertaining to shortages of raw materials, spare parts, etc., with the goal of avoiding bottlenecks and guaranteeing that productive activity remains uninterrupted. These are valid sorts of innovations, but they suffer from poor diffusion and low impact on the generation of new products, processes, or services. They have been stimulated and promoted by several organizations that may coexist within the same enterprise,

such as the Youth Technical Brigades, the Association of Innovators and Rationalizers, and the Forum on Science and Technique.[1]

- Low levels of efficiency and productivity. To exemplify this problem note the continual subsidies to cover losses. In 2014, the year of the latest available data, 151 enterprises recorded losses totaling 439 million pesos. These occurred not only in agricultural enterprises but also in industry (10), tourism (18), etc. (Rodríguez 2015).

The current effort to update the economic model has introduced some modifications in the regulatory framework of state enterprises. For instance, Decree-Law 323/2014 introduced some changes to Decree-Law 28/2007; both of these decree-laws regulate the current System of State Enterprise Administration and Management. The first general point to make about it is that all enterprises, regardless of size, geographic operating area, sector, etc., must use the same system, which in turn is made up of eighteen subsystems. These are characterized by detailed, standardized, and fragmented prescriptions with a functional approach. Excessive documentation is demanded through procedures, manuals, guides, etc., and there is a lack of congruence between these requirements and those of other state entities; further, the requirements have evident omissions in some key areas for competitiveness, including innovation, quality, customer orientation, and strategic management.

With respect particularly to innovation, the first striking fact is that the subsystem denominated "innovation management" says nothing about management and provides no definition of innovation. As a result, the concepts of small improvements or rationalizations are mixed with those of innovation and technological transfer. The system should deal with all of these issues, but it should do so in differentiated form. Articles 495 and 496 of Decree-Law 281/2007 tie the design and implementation of strategic innovation objectives to an excessively bureaucratic treatment; the wording is also ambiguous in terms of what is meant by transfer, assimilation, and generation of technology.

Customer satisfaction is never taken into account, even though meeting needs should be the starting point (see Article 505). To reach that goal, it would be indispensable to assess customers' level of satisfaction, especially when, in Cuba, sales do not constitute an indicator of satisfaction.

Article 493 deals with innovation as an investment in the future, but investments are not approved at the enterprise level. The financial resources for I+D+i lie within the voluntary reserves whose source is the residual enterprise profits after payment of taxes, the creation of compulsory reserves, and a contribution of a return on state investment, which are no less than 50 percent of the gross profit. The creation of this optional reserve must be approved by the Enterprise Group to which the individual enterprise belongs. Moreover, the annual plan is generally not very well supported even though it is imposed from above. It is rigid, of mandatory compliance, and has a time horizon of a single year.

The changes in the regulatory framework introduced in 2014 via several decree-laws and resolutions (see Díaz 2013) deal with social objectives, reducing the number of directive indicators (economic targets that must obligatorily be met), restructuring the enterprise system, redistribution of profits, and wage and salary schemes. The most interesting of these measures is the restructuring. Although the state enterprise is supposedly the fundamental link in the economic chain, it is actually the lowest rung on the ladder of state administration, as evident in Figure 7.1.

Figure 7.1: Institutional Organization

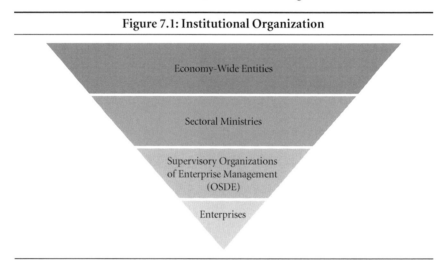

Source: Prepared by the authors from their own research findings and analysis.

Our analysis suggests that all of the inverted pyramid above the enterprise reduces the room for enterprise maneuver and autonomy. The problem lies in the rules and regulations and, in general, in making decisions about some aspects of enterprise management. Thus, such changes as eliminating seven directive indicators or creating new voluntary reserves based on profits do not guarantee autonomy if the enterprises still depend on decisions made at higher levels.

The conceptualization of the new economic and social model (PCC 2016a) contains eight references to innovation, three of which point specifically to the enterprise sector in relation to: innovation-led modernization, encouraging interaction between enterprises and scientific and educational entities, and encouraging interaction with other state and non-state actors. The model emphasizes the need to use informal participatory methods to increase individual and collective incentives for innovation. These, and other more general references to the role of innovation in economic growth and to the state's role in the development of science, technology, and innovation, amount to stating the obvious, though this does not lessen their importance. However, what is most important is whether the model takes into account the aspects of enterprise management that will allow for the development of processes of innovation.

In that regard, the document describes a kind of enterprise management that is subordinate to state decisions under the plan. Autonomy falls within the state regulatory framework and may be exercised to use the profits remaining after the fulfillment of enterprise tax obligations and other commitments to the state. The state also decides the portion devoted to incentives for the workforce and to I+D+i. In this context, then, where do we find autonomy and the authority of the enterprise collectives to make decisions (PCC 2016a)?

Thus, examination of the regulatory conditions influencing enterprise system reveals the following:

- A rigid plan and regulations that do not admit to risks from "the unknown."
- Creativity is not a prioritized trait.
- The regulatory framework encourages a fragmented outlook on the enterprise system, which the manager turns to apply to the enterprise.
- The procedures required by the management system and the plan result in an excess of rules and bureaucracy.
- Customer satisfaction and that of the society do not appear to be priorities of the management and administration system.

Regardless of what goes on in the enterprises, guidelines from the central administration apparatus create conditions for marginal innovations to complement what already exists. This inertial tendency is reinforced by the fact that the organizations are quasi-monopolies, with assured survival and a prevalent "tyranny of supply." The emergence of more entrepreneurial innovation processes with the necessary level of creativity and risk will be very difficult under those conditions. Even routinized innovations characterized by lack of vision, creativity, and risk will be challenging, because having only mechanisms for research and development is not the same as making innovations. Both this framework of enterprise regulation and the conceptualization of the model are contextual elements that decisively influence enterprise performance. Centralized planning as the main means of managing the economy does not incentivize the processes of accumulation, diffusion, and utilization of knowledge as the basis for innovation.

Innovation Processes and Management in State Enterprises: An Approach to a Diagnostic

In this section we seek to portray the response of Cuban state enterprises concerning innovation and its management. A lack of national surveys on innovation activities in state enterprises (the last one was done by the Ministry of Science, Technology, and Environment in 2006 to assess the 2003–2006 period and was released in 2008—see CITMA 2008) leaves us to depend on less far-reaching surveys. These are not statistically representative but do display a certain pattern or regularity in factors pertaining to the task of innovation.

Sixty-four enterprises[2] were surveyed to diagnose the development of innovation processes on the basis of such categories as enterprise strategies and structures, innovation goals and strategies, and conditions for stimulating innovation. These factors are decisive supports for innovation processes; questions were also asked about internal conditions for developing innovations. For the analysis of innovation management, focus groups with management teams from twenty-four enterprises permitted the design of a questionnaire applied to sixty enterprises to identify the main limitations and obstacles.

Diagnostic of Innovation Processes

Evidence from previous studies of innovation in the Cuban state enterprise sector (García and Hernández 2010) reflects the lack of innovation strategies tied to enterprise objectives and strategies, limited access to up-to-date scientific and technological information, and weak links to universities and research centers. Other studies (Díaz 2103, Cazull, Hernández, and Sánchez 2012) also identify difficulties in financing innovation and show the resistance to change within organizations and the excessive centralization that have historically limited initiative and autonomy in the Cuban state socialist enterprise. Table 7.1 summarizes the results of the survey.

Table 7.1: Summary of Diagnostic Results on Innovation Processes: Responses by State Enterprise Managers (Percentages of Total)

STRATEGY & STRUCTURE	**100%**
Enterprise strategy	
Short-term vision is what is most needed to manage in current conditions. It is frequently necessary to privilege the operational sphere, which is a barrier to innovation. Sometimes a working document constitutes a strategy. The search for solutions is usually a response to crisis, not a proactive attitude. The emphasis is on reacting to problems, not foreseeing them.	60%
Enterprise structure	
Structure is hierarchical-functional, not inclined toward creation of networks and cooperation. Rules, procedures, and regulations are very important in management. Excessive structure and excessive rules and regulations occur "very frequently" or "at times."	30%
Other issues	10%
INNOVATION GOALS AND STRATEGIES	
Innovation goals	**100%**
Goals are established in relation to the needs of the productive process,	42%
in relation to the available means and resources,	38%
by officials of higher entities.	18%
Innovation strategy	**100%**
Innovation strategies are oriented toward increasing the internal efficiency of processes,	65%
toward increasing product and service quality,	28%
in response to the needs and expectations of customers.	7%
Conditions for developing innovation processes (1)	
The organizational environment is not very favorable to innovation. Pressures to fulfill the annual plan and specific operational demands by higher entities divert the attention of managers and specialists, reducing the time devoted to innovation management.	86%
The incentive and recognition systems are unfavorable to the development of innovative processes.	82%

Note: The percentages are based on the number of managers responding, N = 104.
Source: Prepared by the authors from their own research findings and analysis.

Pressures to fulfill the annual plan constitute a negative incentive both for innovation and for seeking higher levels of efficiency or effectiveness, because the plan becomes a straitjacket of obligatory fulfillment, imposed from above and usually estranged from the real needs of the enterprise. Certainly, there are innovative top-down directives that emanate from governments, but international practice demonstrates that these are not always the most effective innovations and should not be the only ones pursued. Throughout the enterprise system, the hierarchical structure reproduces the status-quo functioning of the economy, its weak participatory processes, its rejection of new ideas, and other problems.

Because there is no strategy at the enterprise level, the horizon of vision is limited to a single year, as reflected in the plan and in a context where supply rules; both goals and strategies focus on that perspective. It is true that innovations may develop in the short run, but because their application is full of uncertainty and risk for fear that they may jeopardize fulfillment of the plan (with resulting sanctions for managers and wage cuts for workers, since wages are linked to enterprise results), the direction is the opposite of innovation.

Diagnostic of Innovation Management
This diagnostic considers each of the functions of innovation management: vigilance, evaluation, enrichment, optimization and protection. Results appear in Table 7.2.

Table 7.2: Summary of Diagnostic Results on Innovation Management: Vigilance, Evaluation, and Enrichment (Responses by State Enterprise Managers, Percentages of Total)

VIGILANCE	
General absence of systems for monitoring competitors and customers.	92%
Lack of knowledge of market. Lack of market research, which impedes full knowledge of the needs and expectations of the current and potential customers as a source of innovation processes.	56%
EVALUATION	
Insufficient measurement of impacts of innovation processes in enterprises, and poor evaluation of their results. In all the enterprises studied, there were no indicators of the impact of innovation on enterprise performance or on customers.	100%
Lack of normative and methodological bases appropriate to the determination of competitiveness or to differentiating potentials to determine possible strategic directions of innovation for the enterprise.	100%

ENRICHMENT	
Introverted vision with respect to sources that can generate ideas for innovation, with concentration on research and development mechanisms within those enterprises that possess them.	54%
Only at the high levels of enterprise management, with little consideration of customers or important actors in the sector.	28%
Lack of integration of innovation processes with the rest of the processes in the enterprise. All enterprises studied not only lack such integration with their other internal subsystems, but their innovation processes are dispersed among their components, support structures, and documentary base.	100%
In all enterprises, there are weak connections to other actors, especially customers and providers—important sources of innovation—and to universities and research centers, considered important allies in innovation processes.	100%
Limited access to scientific-technical information, which impedes updating of knowledge, identification of trends, and identifying potential state-of-art solutions.	100%
Problems in internal and external communication systems limit acquisition and transmission of knowledge	65%

Note: The percentages are based on the number of managers responding, N = 112.
Source: Prepared by the authors from their own research findings and analysis.

Because of their above-mentioned monopoly character and a general guardedness about the entry of foreign capital, state enterprises are free from the need to monitor competitors and, similarly, from having to take their customers into account. Restricted resources combined with the obligation to fulfill the plan fail to generate incentives for innovations, not even those that could emerge from the development of technological improvements with the functions of optimization and enrichment. These factors limit not only innovation but also productive and effective performance by the enterprises. By way of example, the fulfillment of the requirements of the Forum on Science and Technology, the National Association of Innovators and Rationalizers, and the system of innovation under Decree-Law 281/207 requires the enterprise to separately prepare and submit three different sets of documents that these three sources demand.

In sum, the two diagnostics reveal the following: The environment limits the enterprise's decision-making about its own administration because it imposes a plan that must be strictly followed, as well as patterns of contracting with suppliers and customers; thus, the enterprise becomes an organizational capsule within an inflexible, bureaucratic, and rule-bound structure.

An analysis of the number of patents that Cuba has applied for abroad (an internationally recognized indicator of innovation) shows that on average the number has been low, with a downward trend (see Figure 7.2). Requests for patents in the past seven years have averaged 30 percent of the total from ten years ago; also, 80 percent are concentrated in the biopharmaceutical area.

Figure 7.2: Cuban Applications for International Patents, 1996–2014

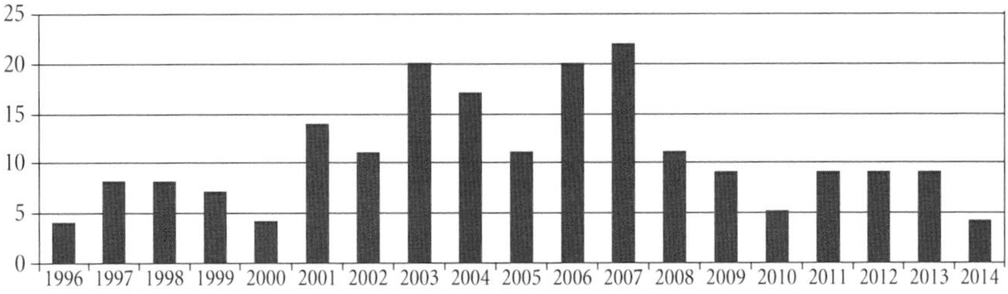

Source: Information received from Oficina Nacional de Marcas y Patentes.

While the conceptualization of the economic and social models addresses how the economy should function, it defines the economy as centralized, planned, and statist in regard to both property and decision-making. There is no discussion of any substantive change in the state enterprises that would demonstrate new incentives or opportunities for innovation in the future.

Final Considerations

Innovation is a key, multi-factor process in the generation of a country's wealth and welfare, its growth and sustainable development. Innovation requires individuals with knowledge, abilities, and the capacity to question reality and break with dogmas. It also requires a culture and leadership oriented in that same direction; infrastructure and resources to support it; consistency among regulations, policies, and interactions; flexible structures; networks of support; and relevant practices and systems inside the enterprise organizations—all of which make innovation a highly complex matter for management.

According to the resolution on the conceptualization of Cuba's economic and social model approved by the April 2016 Party Congress, "Sustainable development of our socialism is possible only through preserving our values and increasing labor productivity so that wealth can grow and be justly distributed, and thus the level and quality of life can do so as well" (PCC 2016d). All of this, as expressed in the resolution on the National Development Plan, should be based on ". . . transformed production and international insertion; infrastructure development; human potential, science, technology, and innovations . . ." (PCC 2016c). Although the existence of a non-state sector has been ratified, the leading role is still conferred on state enterprises as the major generators of wealth and economic growth (Castro 2016).

However, issues discussed throughout this chapter note important limitations to incentivize the role of the state enterprise as a key innovation agent, fundamentally because of factors associated with the regulatory environment, management of the economy, and the state enterprise system, all characterized by excessive centralization, bureaucracy, normative rigidity, and short-term vision. These limitations do not provide state enterprises with incentives to promote innovation, exploit potentials, and interact with other actors (such as providers, customers, and knowledge centers) to implement innovative methods, products, and services that provide more satisfaction to customers and get better economic and financial results.

It is necessary to move more firmly forward in granting powers and responsibilities to state enterprises to make strategic and operational decisions and abandon the approaches that emphasize state tutelage. This would empower these enterprises to become more effective and promote processes of innovation management for which, besides contextual factors, the quality of management and the involvement and competence of human capital are also fundamental.

It is indispensable for the operational mechanisms of the economy to combine adequately plan and market. The plan should guarantee what is strategic for the society. The enterprises should find the pathways of sustainable growth, for which innovation is a central ingredient through the domestic or international markets.

The current homogeneous, rigid and bureaucratic regulatory environment must be lightened to allow enterprises to choose their own forms of management in relation to their characteristics, sectors, and capacities for growth that will help to create conditions in which to develop processes of innovation.

Notes

1. The Youth Technical Brigades are members of a movement for scientific-technical creation and innovation, made up of young people and oriented toward seeking solutions to technical problems in the productive sphere. The Forum is an integrative movement conceived as an organizing tool and incorporated into the System of Science and Technological Innovation; it assesses solutions and proposes the implementation of those deemed most important that promote

import substitution and stimulate the development of technologies and scientific activities that will be decisive for various industries.

2. Of those surveyed, 20 percent were top managers, 50 percent were staff in the offices of quality and innovation, and 30 percent were heads of the departments of quality and innovation.

Bibliography

Alonso, J. A, and J. Triana. 2013. "Nuevas bases para el crecimiento." In *¿Quo Vadis, Cuba? La incierta senda de las reformas*. Madrid: Editorial Catarata.

Blanco, H. 2013. "Gestión de la Innovación en la empresa: Estudios de casos y propuestas de mejoramiento." In *Seminario Anual del Centro de Estudios de la Economía Cubana*. Havana: CEEC.

Blanco, H, and O. Gutiérrez. 2014. "Gestión de la innovación en empresas estatales: asignatura pendiente?" In *Economía Cubana: Transformaciones y Desafíos*, pp. 455–484. Havana: Editorial Ciencias Sociales.

Castro, R. 2016. *Informe Central al Séptimo Congreso del Partido Comunista de Cuba*. http://www.cubadebate.cu/noticias/2016/04/17/informe-central-al-vii-congreso-del-partido-comunista-cuba/#.VyZVqfnhDMw.

Cazull, M., G. Hernández, and N. Sánchez. 2012. "Sistema de Innovación Tecnológica: Estudio de Casos," paper presented at GESTEC 2012. Consulted 10 December at: http://www.gestec.disaic.cu/ponencias_Cuba_2010.htm.

CITMA (Ministerio de Ciencia, Tecnología y Medio Ambiente). 2007. "Propuesta de reglamento para el otorgamiento de la condición de empresa innovadora de la República de Cuba." Havana: Dirección de Política Científica y Tecnológica.

———. 2008. "Segunda encuesta nacional sobre la actividad de innovación. Informe de los resultados 2003–2005." Havana.

Consejo de Ministros. 2007. "Decreto 281 Reglamento para la implantación y consolidación del Sistema de Dirección y Gestión Empresarial Cubano." In *Gaceta Oficial de la República de Cuba*, 17 August.

Díaz, I. 2012. "La productividad en la empresa estatal cubana." In *Economía Cubana, ensayos para una reestructuración necesaria*, pp. 193–221. Havana: IDICT.

———. 2013. "Desafíos de la innovación empresarial en Cuba." In *Seminario Anual del CEEC*. Havana: CEEC.

Díaz, I., and D. Echevarría. 2009. "Análisis del sistema de dirección y gestión empresarial en Cuba: Notas para un debate." In *Seminario Anual del CEEC*. Havana: CEEC.

García, Y., and G. Hernández. 2010. "Caracterización del proceso de innovación en la industria sidero-mecánica de Villa Clara." Presentation at GESTEC. Consulted 10 December 2012 at http://www.gestec.disaic.cu/ponencias-Cuba_2010.htm.

Gutiérrez, O. 2013. "Reflexiones sobre los ambientes de innovación en las empresas cubanas." In *Seminario Anual del CEEC*. Havana: CEEC.

Guzmán, J. 2006. "El rol del emprendimiento en el crecimiento económico." In *Estudios de Economía Aplicada*, Volume 24–2:361–387.

Hamel, G., and C. K. Prahalad. 1999. *La gestión en la incertidumbre.* Madrid: Ediciones Deusto.

Marcelo, L. 2011. "Separación de funciones estatales y empresariales: problema estratégico principal de la economía cubana." In *Cuba: Investigación económica,* 1–2, January-December.

Ministerio de Finanzas y Precios. 2014. "Resolución 203 Procedimiento para el Sistema de Relaciones Financieras entre las empresas estatales y las sociedades mercantiles ciento por cinto (100%) cubanas." In *Gaceta Oficial de la Repuública de Cuba,* 28 April.

ONEI. 2009. *Anuario estadístico de Cuba.* Havana.

———. 2012. *Anuario estadístico de Cuba.* Havana.

———. 2014. *Anuario estadístico de Cuba.* Havana.

OCDE (Organización para la Cooperación del Desarrollo Económico). 2005a. "La gestión de la innovación como herramienta para la competitividad." Consulted 15 April 2013 at http://www.oece.org/trabajos34/innovacion-competitividad.

———. 2005b. *Manual de Oslo. Guía para la recogida e interpretación de datos sobre innovación.* Paris: Ediciones OCDE. [English translation from http://www.oecd-ilibrary.org/.]

PCC (Partido Comunista de Cuba). 2011. *Lineamientos de la Política Económica y Social del Partido y la Revolución.* Havana: Editora Política.

———. 2016a. *Conceptualización del Modelo Económico y Social de Desarrollo Socialista.* Havana: tabloid edition.

———. 2016b. *Resolución sobre Resultados de la Implementación de los Lineamientos de la Política Económica y Social del Partido y la Revolución, aprobados en el VI Congreso y su actualización para el período 2016–2021.* http://www.cubadebate.cu/especiales/2016/04/18/resolucion-sobre-resultados-de-la-implementacion-de-los-lineamientos-de-la-politica-economica-y-social-del-partido-y-la-revolucion-aprobados-en-el-vi-congreso-y-su-actualizacion-el-periodo-2016-2021/#.VyYcLnrnFNs.

———. 2016c. *Resolución sobre el Plan Nacional de Desarrollo Económico y Social hasta 2030: Propuesta de visión de la nación, ejes y sectores estratégicos.* http://www.cubadebate.cu/especiales/2016/04/18/resolucion-sobre-el-plan-nacional-de-desarrollo-economico-y-social-hasta-2030-propuesta-de-vision-de-la-nacion-ejes-y-sectores-estrategicos/#.VyYcOXrnFNs.

———. 2016d. *Resolución sobre el Proyecto de Conceptualización del Modelo Económico y Social Cubano de Desarrollo Socialista.* http://www.cubadebate.cu/especiales/2016/04/18/resolucion-sobre-el-proyecto-de-conceptualizacion-del-modelo-economico-y-social-cubano-de-desarrollo-socialista/#.VyYcQXrnFNs.

Pérez, C. 2000. "Cambio de paradigma y rol de la tecnología en el desarrollo." Presented at the MCT's Foro de Apertura del Ciclo 'La ciencia y la tecnología en la construcción del futuro del país,' Caracas, June. www.carlotaperez.org/downloads /pubs/CP-Foro-MCT.pdf.

————. 2013. "Bases para la actualización de la metodología para la elaboración del plan en condiciones de unificación monetaria." Dissertation presented for Diplomado de Administración Pública, Havana, November.

RICYT. 2001. *Manual de Bogotá. Normalización de indicadores de innovación tecnológica en América Latina.* Bogotá: RICYT / OEA / CYTED. [English translation from http://www.ricyt.org/manuales/doc_view/149-bogota-manual, p 47.]

Rodríguez, J. L. 2015. "Cuba y la compleja transformación de la empresa estatal III." In *Cubadebate*, 7 January. Consulted 9 February 2016 at http://www.cubadebate.cu/especiales/2015/01/07Cuba-desempeño-economico-2014-y-proyecciones-2015-i/.

Schumpeter, J. A. 1935. "The analysis of economic change." In *Review of Economic Statistics*. Volume 17:2–10.

Schwab, K. 2014. Speech at the presentation of the Global Competitiveness Report, World Economic Forum, Davos, Switzerland, 2 February. Consulted 5 February, 2014, at http://www.americaeconomia.com/informe-de-competitividad-global-2013-2014.

Yoguel, G. 2000. "Creación de competencias en ambientes locales y redes productivas." In *Revista CEPAL*, Number 71:105–119.

8

Cuba: Notes on Multilateral External Financing

Marlén Sánchez Gutiérrez

The process of updating the Cuban economic model has required rethinking Cuba's insertion into international financial markets. Although attention has centered on the generation of incentives to attract private funds through Direct Foreign Investment (DFI), there have also been encouraging steps to strengthen the mobilization of official resources.

Since the first decade of this century, the attempt to normalize relations with creditors in bilateral fashion—and, since 2013, within the framework of the Paris Club—has proved essential to attract DFI, access new lines of credit, and diversify bilateral sources of official financing.

Meanwhile, since 2013, Cuba has been in conversation with the Development Bank of Latin America (Corporación Andina de Fomento, CAF after its Spanish acronym). These talks led to the signing of a first collaboration accord on September 2, 2016, with the goal of creating financial mechanisms favorable to Cuban economic and social development, promotion of technical cooperation between the two parties, and Cuba's future entry as a shareholder in CAF. Such action would allow for progress toward integration into the regional and international arena and offer the possibility of accessing multilateral capital flows.

Additionally, in academic circles a discussion has developed regarding the advisability of Cuban membership in international financial institutions (IFIs), as well as about the contribution that such bodies, at least the multilateral development banks, could make to the development of productive investment in Cuba.

In these pages I will consider the advisability of a Cuban relationship with IFIs through a cost-benefit analysis. For a comparative view, I will synthesize some of the experiences of China, Vietnam, and Russia in the use of such institutions, deriving some lessons for Cuba, before offering some closing thoughts to enrich the discussion under way in academic circles.

A Cuban Return to the International Monetary Fund and World Bank: Pros and Cons

The advisability of Cuba's return to the Bretton Woods institutions may be discussed from two different but not mutually exclusive perspectives. One is influenced primarily by the direction that participants foresee in the process of transforming the Cuban economic model, and that direction's consistency with the nature and approach of the IMF and the World Bank. The other starting point is linked to the restrictions imposed by the U.S. economic and financial blockade imposed to prevent Cuban membership in these institutions.

In general, those who believe that Cuba is in transition "toward a capitalist model" see its seeking access to IFIs as inevitable, given those institutions' orientation toward a market economy and their neoliberal bias. Those who foresee the creation of a Chinese-style "market socialist" model also lean toward Cuba's entry because the multilateral institutions could prove useful at particular moment and in specific contexts; this is the position held by the author of this paper. Conversely, those who reject Cuba's return to such institutions believe that it is incompatible for a socialist country to be a member of such absolutely neoliberal institutions with their strong tendency to offer recommendations about economic policy that have doubtful effectiveness and a high social cost.

The ideological rejection in the name of socialism raises the question of whether China and Vietnam were mistaken when they joined such institutions. However, independently of the marked differences or hegemonic intentions of these two countries, they have not fared poorly thus far.

It is true that "in the Chinese case . . . the arrangements with the IMF have been of a very different type, largely directed toward strengthening its presence within the framework of the major international financial institutions, something totally consistent with China's strategic projection as a global power." It is also true "that there are different possible levels of dealing with the IMF, within which Cuba's, clearly, would be one of 'playing in the minor leagues'" (Monreal 2015, 2). However, my purpose is to derive some lessons and find the most useful manner of using the IMF as a doorway into the World Bank. This implies membership while avoiding the situation of having to negotiate with the IMF—or, if negotiation becomes necessary, knowing how to do so from the "minor leagues" with the same principled integrity that Cuba maintained for fifty-eight years. Cuba should anticipate and prepare for such possibilities because any negotiation with the Fund would be political, and thus would involve a typical power relationship.

There is a relatively broad consensus that "Cuba needs international economic insertion in general, and the financial sort in particular, to support the efforts now under way and to contribute to shorten the time needed for the recovery of the national economy . . ." (García 2012, 2). However, less consensus exists about what type of international insertion is desirable. "It is not just any insertion; it is not one that follows worn-out patterns that have demonstrated their ineffectiveness, nor frameworks that tend toward intolerable conditions. . . . In the transformations under way, the objective must be development, with economic growth as one of the means and with international insertion and cooperation as a functional contributor to the project and model, not the other way around" (García 2012, 2).

Opinions vary widely, to wit:

"The new openings in United States policy . . . are reshaping both the bilateral relationship and Cuba's international insertion. Isolation is more and more a policy of the past; Cuba, the United States, and the international financial institutions must adapt to this reality. To achieve that, each one needs to rethink the worn-out policies that have lasted for decades. In the new context, joining the IFIs is a critical step in the long-term movement toward full economic reintegration." (Vidal 2015, 8)

"The recent historical experience of the transition to capitalism in the formerly socialist countries of eastern Europe shows the enormous social cost of neoliberal adjustment programs that accept the prescriptions of the IMF. Updating the Cuban economic model has called for an objective recognition of the market and non-state property as elements that can—under state control—favor a more efficient economy, alongside essential transformations in public property in a process of transition toward a prosperous and sustainable socialism. This is a difficult process, complex and even painful, because it imposes costs in the cause of a better future and it is subject—like any other human endeavor—to errors that may be committed." (Rodríguez 2015, 12–13)

This overall discussion is complex and requires a variety of readings from the points of view of political economy and of the theoretical conception of the Bretton Woods institutions, which extend beyond the goals of this chapter. In the Seventh Congress of the Cuban Communist Party, the continuity of socialism in Cuba was made clear: "The principal lines of our work will emerge, directed toward achieving a sovereign, independent, socialist, prosperous and sustainable nation." (Partido Comunista de Cuba 2016, 6). That makes the first of the outlined perspectives particularly polemical.

The other facet of the issue is much simpler, starting from the assumption that the island's entry into the IFIs depends on the lifting of the U.S. blockade and the restrictions imposed by the Helms-Burton Act that excluded Cuba from multilateral financing. In fact, the impossibility of accessing such resources has been one of the arguments put forward by Cuban authorities in the reports on the blockade they have presented annually at the United Nations during votes on the Resolution titled, "The need to put an end to the economic, trade and financial blockade imposed by the United States of America against Cuba."

Thus the initial question becomes: is Cuba not a member of the IMF and the World Bank because it is a socialist country, or because of the restrictions imposed by the U.S. blockade? Although the answer involves a little of each (Cuba does not want to, but the United States also does not allow it, and now Cuba wants to, but the United States still does not allow it), my main focus is on the second part of the question, because of the change in the context of the relations between Cuba and the United States and the speed at which that change unfolded thus far.

If it is assumed that the obstacle lies in the blockade, then in a context of increasing flexibility or eventual lifting of that impediment, what would remain is political decision-making; at that juncture, it would help for the Cuban government to be prepared to make a cost-benefit analysis of what a relationship with the Bretton Woods institutions would bring. The process of normalization of relations between Cuba and the United States will be complicated by the significant differences between the two countries and by the great uncertainty surrounding the Trump administration, but it appears that Cuba is closer to the end of the blockade than to its start.

What are, then, the advantages and disadvantages of being a member of these institutions, what opportunities do they offer, what risks do they carry, how should Cuba prepare to negotiate with the institutions, and how should it approach the issue of their setting conditions? Consideration of such membership requires time to change mentalities and approach the topic from a pragmatic position yet one that upholds Cuban sovereignty in the design of a development strategy. After so many years of not depending on the IFIs, is it possible to use them in a way that favors our national interest—to do so with discretion, trying to find the right niches and opportunities and to avoid questions of principle that would damage our sovereign decision-making?

Among the various reasons why Cuba's membership in the Bretton Woods institutions would be advantageous are those put forward in several works by Pujol and by Feinberg. These can be synthesized as:

1. The need to break with economic and financial isolation. The IMF and the World Bank are not exactly the paradigm for the multilateral credit-issuing bodies Cuba needs, but there are no others at the global level that play a similar role. The IMF and the World Bank include 188 member states and constitute specialized agencies of the United Nations system of which Cuba is a part. It is true that their policies have a marked neoliberal bias, but the fundamental issue is one of international financial inclusion. Cuba is a founder of the General Agreement on Tariffs and Trade (GATT) and a member of the World Trade Organization (WTO) and has dealt for many years with the contradictions of the world trade system, including its growing complexity, asymmetries, and inequitable distribution of the supposed benefits to be expected from trade liberalization.

2. The benefits of gaining a guarantor of access to international capital markets and a facilitator in the processes of debt renegotiation, another function carried out by the IMF. Earlier in this decade, Cuba renegotiated the part of its passive debt that pertains to the Paris Club without IMF mediation. Certainly, one reading of this fact would be that Cuba can do without the IMF in its future renegotiations within the Paris Club framework.

   However, a new factor was the significant influence that the new relations between Cuba and the United States had in the achievement of the agreement with the Paris Club. The majority of Paris Club members were disposed to show flexibility toward Cuba because of their growing interest in conducting business on the island after a thaw in its relation with the United States. That is, a particular constellation of events favored an unprecedented renegotiation, and it also sent an interesting signal about the possible U.S. attitude toward a future Cuban bid for membership in the IMF.

3. The possibility of access to multilateral resources (financial and otherwise) that are, technically, less costly than private ones.

4. The desirability of channeling compensatory financing to deal with disequilibria in the balance of the payments (in the case of the IMF) and also investment resources to stimulate development (from the institutions that make up the World Bank) (Pujol, 66). Because there is a parallelism between the two institutions, such that to become a

member of the World Bank it is compulsory to be a prior member of
the IMF, Cuba must inevitably consider a future relationship with the
Fund if it wants to get access to the resources of the Bank.

5. The option to compensate for a lack of benefits in terms of official
   development aid, given that the conditions of multilateral financing (interest rates and repayment schedules) are the most favorable
   within the ambit of financing flows. If Cuba cannot receive foreign
   aid funds because it is categorized as a middle-income country, then
   access to these multilateral funds would offer an opportunity to
   acquire less costly financing.

6. Sharing social projects in which Cuba has accumulated experience
   and international recognition. Also, membership would be an excellent opportunity for an accounting of Cuba's international cooperation with other countries, which does not appear in the statistics of
   South-South cooperation.

Countering these benefits are costs associated (from the Cuban perspective) with the commitments assumed upon joining such institutions.
Those commitments could be widely questioned. The most sensitive issues
in a relationship between Cuba and the IFIs would be:

1. Accepting the obligations of the IMF's Articles of Agreement, particularly Articles IV and VIII. Article IV, Obligations Regarding Exchange
   Arrangements, discusses these obligations, their supervision, and the
   question of parities and the currency circulating in the given country (IMF 2011, 5–7). Article VIII, General Obligations of Members,
   discusses the obligation to avoid discriminatory payment rates and
   monetary practices. This Article lays out rules related to convertibility
   of funds held by other member countries, information that must be
   supplied to the Fund, consultation between member countries about
   existing international agreements, and the obligation to collaborate
   regarding reserve asset policies (IMF 2–11. 24–27). Currently Cuba
   has a WTO waiver pertaining to the definition and management of
   exchange rates. Not being a member of the Fund, it is not subject to
   that institution's supervision and thus to the examination of its trade
   policies, which exempts Cuba from discussion about unfair international trade practices through currency manipulations—in this case,
   unchanging and fixed rates and overvaluation.

2. The requirement to share statistical information needed to harmo-
   nize the data bases used in studies, research, and policy design, as
   well the requirement to review some of the methodologies used to

compile national accounts. The availability of information has always been a highly sensitive topic for Cuba, where economic statistics, particularly monetary and financial ones, have long been treated with a high degree of confidentiality. The most convincing reason given for Cuba's confidentiality practices has been the restrictions imposed by the U.S. blockade, which assumes surveillance of the flow of funds, freezing of bank accounts related to operations with Cuba, and the need to protect investors who operate in the country in spite of the blockade. In this context, the most prudent course was to hide the information in order to avoid additional pressures. However, Cuba is likely to begin to make its information more available, for two reasons. The first is the commitments assumed in the renegotiation with the Paris Club, which oblige the country to inform its creditors annually about the performance of the Cuban economy. While this information could remain within the confines of confidentiality, it is also true that the Paris Club has its own transparency policy, and contradictions between Cuba's and the Paris Club may emerge. The second reason stems from the 2030 Agenda for Sustainable Development, which identifies more than 300 indicators to measure the fulfillment of the seventeen Sustainable Development Objectives, which in turn comprise 169 goals (United Nations 2015, 11–22). This will oblige Cuba to supply the information that allows for monitoring the fulfillment of these commitments.

3. Consent to IMF monitoring and supervision as part of the exercise of consultation required by Article IV. Fund directors carry out annual visits to member countries to review economic performance, after which they write a report to submit to the Board of Governors. If important risks are observed—for the nation, the region, or the international financial system—then recommendations are formulated that the implicated countries must follow. It is improbable, in the short run, that Cuba would accept such "intromission" during a time of changes and redefinition of its policies and strategies, particularly given the asymmetries that have characterized IMF supervision.

4. The IMF quota. As long as the problem of the dual currency and dual exchange system in Cuba is not resolved—a process that is proceeding much more slowly than anticipated—it will be very difficult to measure Cuba's economic performance and even more so to compare it that of other countries. Without an economically justified exchange rate, there is the risk of overestimating certain results while underestimating others, and this would create technical problem when it comes

to calculating Cuba's IMF quota. Also, there is the issue of Cuba's methodology to calculate its GDP, which differs from the internationally accepted method; this discrepancy can in turn generate distortion. "To make comparisons possible, some kind of preparatory work would be needed to re-estimate Cuba's accounts in accordance with the international standard. The system of dual exchange rates also generates technical difficulties in estimating national income and comparing it with that of other countries; as a result, Cuba's published national income estimate may be over-estimated, and so may be the calculation of its quota" (Pujol 2012, 65). Still, it is expected that the process of currency and exchange rate unification will be completed long before Cuba decides whether or not to join the Bretton Woods institutions, so part of this problem will probably be alleviated.

5. Conditionality of financing. This is doubtless the main obstacle to be overcome because it is a highly sensitive political issue. The IMF has been heavily criticized for the excessive conditions of its loans, involving recommendations for austerity programs of dubious effectiveness in promoting economic growth and financial stability, yet creating a great social impact.

Despite the attempts to rationalize such conditionality and focus it toward areas strictly within the authority of the IMF, since the first revision of the Guidelines for Conditionality was adopted in March 2001 (IMF 2002, 6), these have only increased in both quantitative and qualitative terms. A 2014 study by Eurodad, the European Network on Debt and Development, calculated an average of 19.5 conditions per program, representing a significant increase in comparison with a previous study that found an average of 13.7 structural conditions per program in the 2005–2007 period, and 14 in 2003–2004 (Griffiths and Todoulos 2014, 4).

In considering membership, Cuba would have to consider the structural conditions that tie Fund financing to the implementation of reforms in the receiving countries' legislative and institutional policies (Griffiths and Todoulos 2014, 7). These policy changes still center around limiting fiscal space by reducing governments' ability to make decisions about the management of spending and revenue, and they continue to focus mainly on sensitive economic areas such as liberalization and privatization. Implementation of the adjustment programs requires important policy changes that certainly go beyond the range of the IMF's original mandate and that should be the exclusive prerogatives of governments. Nonetheless, it would be opportune to take a look at the juridical nature of this conditionality so as to know how to approach it.

First, the adjustment program is negotiated with the authorities of the country soliciting financing; thus the stance taken by that country's administration toward the Fund is key. Of course, the circumstances in which IMF aid is solicited are also an essential factor; the same country in difficult circumstances can accept conditions that in better circumstances it would not accept; this all depends on the country's need for resources and its access to alternative sources of financing, yet the point is that there is always some room for negotiation. What happens in practice in that this conditionality has expressed a power relationship that, in the final analysis, reflects the asymmetries that prevail inside the IMF. As Paul Volcker said on one occasion, "When the Fund consults with a poor and weak country, the country gets in line. When it consults with a big and strong country, the Fund gets in line" (Buira 2003). Cuba will have to learn from the experience of poor and weak countries how to avoid falling into the trap of conditionality.

Second, the IMF has specific guidelines for applying conditionality (see IMF 2002, 1–6), but it doesn't always follow them, particularly those related to the need to take into account the domestic political and social objectives of the member countries, as well as the non-imposition of conditions of an essentially political nature. Knowledge of the IMF's own regulations in this regard is essential not only during the process of negotiation of an adjustment program but throughout the period of relationship. Such knowledge is a part of the rights of member countries, and that right should be exercised.

Third, while a letter of intent signed by countries receiving Fund financing constitutes the juridical expression of an adjustment program, technically it is not a legal contract, so there is no legal obligation to fulfill the agreement. It is a unilateral decision by the Fund, not a legal agreement between Fund and the member country (Leckow 2002). Thus the legal consequences associated with failure of or non-compliance with an adjustment program are minimized. This is a resource that can be wielded in favor of the borrower.

Likewise, if in the negotiation of an adjustment program a country accepts conditions that cannot be implemented because they would strangle the nation or set goals that are too ambitious for the short and medium range, nothing legally binds the authorities to continue that program. They may abandon it and opt for a restructuring that obviously would bring new challenges but that would be less costly than to continue staying trapped in the inertia of the adjustment program. In fact, the country can have recourse to solidly challenging the legitimacy and legality of part of the debt from the standpoint of international law, as well as arguing that the IMF has violated its own statutes. Mounting such a challenge is a sovereign decision on the part of the receiver of the loan, determined by its own government.

In the case of the World Bank, these costs may be simplified by the nature of that institution and the distance that has opened in recent years between its policies and those of the IMF. However, IMF requirements must nevertheless be confronted because membership in the Bank depends on membership in the Fund. The history of these institutions shows that in some periods, such as the 1980s and part of the 1990s, the IMF's stabilization policies were interwoven with the structural adjustment policies of the Bank, reinforcing the ties between the two institutions. The IMF became involved in the sphere of action of the World Bank and vice versa, generating a double conditionality that nearly asphyxiated debtor economies. By the mid-'90s they had parted ways again, with the Bank returning to its role as a development bank, while its financing politics began to focus more on poverty, the environment, and social issues, so that institution has been somewhat "de-satanized."

Looking Toward Other Multilateral Development Banks

Cuba may also consider access to IFIs by way of other multilateral development banks. Cuba's ties with CAF came about through the interest of both parties, not just Cuba's; this joint interest intensified after the change in U.S.-Cuban relations announced on December 17, 2014. Similar factors pertain to Cuba's relationship with the Inter-American Development Bank (IDB). The IDB is designed to deal with the specific problems of Latin America. Knowing the region's particulars, it is easier for the IDB to identify investment possibilities and to carry out regulation and supervision. The IDB could also contribute to confronting several of the challenges facing the Cuban financial system, from currency unification to expanding the microfinance sector.

One obstacle to Cuba's entry into the IDB is, once again, the U.S. blockade. Title 1, Section 104, of the Helms-Burton Act explicitly states that the term "international financial institution" applies to the IMF, the International Bank for Reconstruction and Development (IBRD, the World Bank's formal name), the International Development Association, the International Finance Corporation, the Multilateral Investment Guaranty Agency, and the Inter-American Development Bank (Helms-Burton 1996, 12).

Another obstacle is that the IDB's Articles of Agreement state that its members must belong to the Organization of American States (OAS).

Cuba's exclusion from the OAS was suspended in 2009, but the island is not inclined to accept the conditions in terms of democracy demanded for its re-entry. Still, it is possible to apply for the status of observer. This would be a technically feasible option at least in an initial period. An inclination to accept Cuba on the part of the IDB has been visible for some time, long before December 17, 2014.

In sum, Cuba should carry out a cost-benefit analysis and assess whether it should join the IFIs as an observer or a member. In the changing context between Cuba and the United States, exploring an approach to the IDB, the World Bank, and the IMF should be on the agenda of the Cuban government, though these might happen at different times. This is the moment to anticipate, prepare, and see what can be accepted and what must necessarily be rejected in any future relationship. Clearly, these are functional institutions for capitalist economies, but they are also proving functional for so-called socialist economies.

Technical vs. Financial Assistance: Some Experiences with the IMF and the World Bank

In order to approach the issue objectively and to be able to identify the major benefits and ways to minimize the costs, it is best to understand that the IFIs differ from one to another and therefore so does the financing they offer. In any attempt to consider an overture to these institutions, each one should be evaluated separately.

The IMF, in practice, functions as a lender of last resort. Its financing is compensatory, used to address disequilibria in member countries' balance of payments. The World Bank is a development bank (along with the IDB and CAF); it offers investment financing, including financing for social development projects. However, the role of these institutions cannot be reduced exclusively to channeling financial resources; they also play an important part in capacity building, identification and promotion of investment opportunities, and the transfer of knowledge and experience in their respective spheres of action.

In this context, in the short and medium run Cuba's main benefits from a relationship with the IMF and the World Bank could result from technical cooperation. Knowledge transfers, exchange of experiences, and generation of new capacities all contribute to developing more effective regulatory frameworks and institutions; they can also help in drawing lessons about what pitfalls should be avoided. Such transfer and exchange take place through various modalities: training in financial and macro-economic issues, workshops, seminars, courses, research projects, and policy advice. In the case of the IMF, technical assistance is administered from its Washington headquarters and carried out through a broad network consisting of its Institute for Capacity Development, regional centers, assistance programs, specific funds, and other activities supported by bilateral donors.

The IMF Institute for Capacity Development publishes an annual catalog with detailed descriptions of its proposed programs for the coming year; these are systematically revised in accord with the needs of those receiving the service. The catalog summarizes not only the training offered by the international headquarters but also that of the regional centers. Two of these centers are located in Latin America and the Caribbean, thereby deserving a closer look. These are the IMF's Regional Centers for Technical Assistance: one for Central America, Panama, and the Dominican Republic, founded in 2009, and another for the Caribbean, serving twenty Caribbean nations, founded in 2001 in Barbados (IMF 2010, 9).

These centers, providing aid at the regional and national level, have become important vehicles for channeling resources to IMF member countries and also for coordinating policies, statistics, and regulatory frameworks on a regional scale. Further, they create important synergies with other donors, all of which allows for better coordination of aid. In general, they provide specialized training on macroeconomic and financial affairs, grouped into three large areas: fiscal issues, monetary and financial issues, and statistical techniques. "[These include] topics of vital interest for the reform process in Cuba: macroeconomic analysis, tax and customs administration, public finance management, economic statistics, and regulation and supervision of the financial sector and capital markets. Training for mid-level technical staff will be vital for stimulating Cuban governmental institutions at various levels—local, provincial, and national" (Feinberg 2012b, 10). Likewise, Lorenzo Pérez points out that "in current Cuban economic conditions, the country would very much benefit from returning to the institution . . . Cuba would receive technical assistance in improving the country's economic institutions; there is a rich field of knowledge from which the country can benefit" (Pérez 2016, 6).

Within this wide range of possible kinds of capacity building, the objective is to evaluate what would turn out to be useful for Cuba. Within these available modalities, training and skill-building clearly make more sense for Cuba than policy advice. In terms of topics, the priorities could be statistical techniques, financial programming, information technologies and communications, financial software, etc. There is a large field of international methodology for compiling data related to balance of payments, public finance, and the real sector of the economy; Cuba could become engaged in this discussion and even socialize its own statistical compilation methodologies. At the same time, as a result of the limitations within which the Cuban financial system has had to operate, the country has significant needs in terms of knowledge, use, and practice of the most sophisticated information technologies; this could serve as another point of entry.

Following this logic, it would also be useful to assess the experiences of China, Vietnam, and Russia in dealing with both the financial and the non-financial resources of the IMF and the World Bank. Though tackling that subject in all its dimensions is beyond the confines of this chapter, certain elements are worth discussing here.

China is a founding member of both institutions, but it has made use of the Fund's financial resources on only two occasions. In 1981, by way of a standby agreement, it received 450 million Special Drawing Rights (SDRs), and in 1986 it received another disbursement of 597.7 SDR. Both credits were repaid without great stress (IMF 2016a, 1). In contrast, cooperation involving technical assistance has grown substantially since 1990 through visits of experts, exchanges of delegations, and seminars. These have focused on the areas of fiscal policy and tax administration; trade policy; banking legislation; development of monetary instruments; inter-bank markets; convertibility of both current and capital/financing accounts; unification of currency exchange markets; and economic and financial statistics. The main training programs requested by Chinese officials have been in the field of financial programming and analysis, as well as methodological designs for compiling balance of payment and public finance statistics.

As for the World Bank, China has shown great ability to make use of its resources, having become its third most important borrower. From 1981 to today, China has registered a total of 543 projects with the World Bank Group, encompassing 365 with the IBRD, 71 with the International Development Association (IDA, the World Bank's concessional lender), and 107 with other institutions of the Group. The level of dropped projects is low, only eighteen in the entire period, which is slightly over 3 percent; 405 projects have ended while 107 are active (BM 2017a, 1). In terms of sectoral distribution, China has followed the priorities set through its development strategy. It has channeled significant resources to develop its public administration, including government administration at the central and subnational levels. It has also prioritized issues regarding water supply, purification, and flood control; environment, energy, and electricity; agriculture; transportation infrastructure (roads and railroads); and social services.

Vietnam joined the IMF in 1956, and since 1990 it requested financial assistance on three occasions, for smaller sums than China. It reached a standby agreement in 1993 for 145 million SDR; in 1994 it was issued another credit associated with old structural adjustment programs totaling 362.4 million SDR; finally in 2001 it signed an agreement to stimulate growth and reduce poverty worth 290 million SDR (IMF 2016b, 1). Vietnam has no delayed payments or pending debt.

The Fund's technical assistance to Vietnam grew during the country's second period of Socialist Renewal, characterized by encouraging a socialist-oriented market economy through transforming existing state enterprises, banks, and investments. Cooperation has been channeled from IMF central headquarters and from its regional centers, directed at the areas of public spending administration, tax policy, fiscal transparency, monetary and exchange operations, central banking, bank reconstruction and supervision, economic statistics, etc. Vietnamese officials have been offered training in financial analysis, monetary programming, public finance, balance of payments methodology, and government financial statistics. Additionally, there have been specific seminars on centrally planned economies in transition.

Vietnam's relations with the World Bank have been very different from China's. Because of its income level, Vietnam's strongest ties have been with the IDA; being its sixth largest borrower, the country has enjoyed the most favorable IDA concessional privileges. From 1978 to the present, Vietnam has registered 254 projects with the World Bank Group, 160 of them with the IDA, 19 with the IBRD, and 75 with agencies of the World Bank group. Of the total, 59 are active and only 7 dropped, showing the lowest rate of dropped projects of the three countries under examination in this chapter section (BM 2017a, 1). For Vietnam, the industrial sector has been the priority; the bulk of projects have been directed toward stimulating that decisive branch of its economy. In order of priority, industry is followed by public administration and social services. Other areas of attention have included water supply, purification, and flood control, as well as environmental and energy issues.

In contrast, Russia offers an example of what not to do. Unlike China and Vietnam, Russia's relationship with the IMF has been highly questionable. During the 1990s it depended exclusively on the Fund to monitor its transition to capitalism at a very high social cost. The adjustment programs recommended by the Fund took a long time to achieve macroeconomic stabilization, and the privatization process was a failure. Rather than designing a general and gradual strategy of institutional development, the authorities imposed a radical reform based on the same formulae that the Fund had recommended in Latin America in 1980s, which ended up dragging Russia into a wave of crises in the 1990s. In order to compensate for some of these costs, from 1992 to 1999 each and every year the IMF disbursed billions of SDRs to Russia's general resource account at the IMF. Repurchases began in 1996 and lasted until 2005. During Russia's financial crisis in 1998, IMF credit alone exceeded 13 billion SDR (IMF 2015b, 1).

With the World Bank Group, Russia's strategy was more consistent, although the country has displayed problems in maintaining the continuity of projects that were considered priorities at a given moment. The strongest ties have been with the IBRD, with which almost all projects have been created. From 1993 to date, Russia registered 117 projects with the World Bank Group, of which 68 have closed and only 10 are still active. The rate of dropped projects has been high, around 25 percent of the total registered in that period. In sectoral terms, Russia's priority has been to focus on the area of public administration and government, fundamentally at the national level; it has also channeled resources to social services, the energy sector, the environment, and electricity generation (BM 2017c, 1).

In sum, at least five lessons can be drawn from this review of the ties of China, Vietnam, and Russia with the Bretton Woods institutions:

- Discretion in the use of IMF's financial resources reduces uncertainty concerning the Fund's interference in a country's domestic affairs. It is neither desirable nor advisable to become a chronic borrower, which in turn suggests the importance of securing alternative sources of multilateral financing. In this context, regional financial cooperation alternatives are becoming quite feasible, especially in Asia.
- Technical assistance becomes useful if the receiving country can blend it into its national development strategy, and if it can occur through modalities and around issues that truly contribute to generate knowledge and capacities and to increase effectiveness in the design and implementation of national policies.
- Prioritize the resources of the World Bank. Accord primacy to finance activities related to the public sector and government instead of promoting the private sector, thereby making it possible to promote "public goods" that serve the general interest.
- Take advantage of the World Bank's accumulated experience in projects focused on the energy sector, the environment, highway infrastructure, agriculture, and water treatment.

- Design a differentiated strategy for relations with the different institutions that make up the World Bank Group in accordance with development needs and national priorities.

Closing Thoughts

It is worth looking at two different paths forward: one is tactical, focused on an approach to the multilateral development banks (CAF, IBD, World Bank), and the other is strategic, addressing how to create the bases for a future relationship with the IMF.

With CAF, a path is already open. The collaboration agreement between the two parties represents a first step toward the development of shared agendas, although Cuba is not yet a CAF member. The good news is that the CAF can offer support through third parties or non-governmental organizations such as green funds, which promote the use and spread of clean energy sources. This is very positive because it would allow Cuba to access financing that would contribute to the development of priority sectors as defined in its national economic and social development plan for 2030, such as renewable energy.

The equation is more complex with the other institutions; the variables in play are essentially political, both from the Cuban side and from that of the United States:

Entry into the IDB depends on Cuba's membership in the OAS and the lifting or loosening of the U.S. blockade. While Cuba's return to the OAS requires only a Cuban political decision, the lifting of the blockade is a prerogative of the government of the United States.

Further, to join the World Bank a country must be a member of the IMF, and if one assumes that the U.S. blockade is major obstacle to Cuba's entry into these organizations, then in the absence of the blockade that decision comes to depend only on Cuba, which nevertheless could not say "yes" to the World Bank and "no" to the IMF. Thus the dependent and independent variables of the equation overlap, which makes the panorama more complex.

If the variables at play are essentially political, a pragmatic point of departure would be to de-ideologize the issue and think about how to maximize benefits and manage costs. In that sense, joining the IDB could be a first step, while exploring the possibilities of the World Bank mindful that the IMF is the gate for entry. It is in principle possible to receive technical assistance from the World Bank and the IMF without being a member of those institutions, except that the Helms-Burton Act is very clear when it says:

If any international financial institution approves a loan or other assistance to the Cuban Government over the opposition of the United States, then the Secretary of the Treasury shall withhold from payment to such institution an amount equal to the amount of the loan or other assistance, with respect to either of the following types of payment:

1. The paid-in portion of the increase in capital stock of the institution.
2. The callable portion of the increase in capital stock of the institution (Helms-Burton 1996, 12).

In a context of loosening or elimination of the U.S. blockade, this obstacle would disappear, and Cuba, without being a member of those institutions, could explore relationships with them through some of the modalities described in the experiences of China and Vietnam but adapted to its own reality and interests. The key idea is that, before Cuba were to join the IMF and World Bank, it should already have alternative sources of multilateral financing and enough experience in the use of the financial and non-financial resources of those institutions.

Also, it is necessary to coherently integrate Cuba's international financial insertion with the challenges facing its own financial system. Though it is impossible to calculate in advance the potential impacts of currency unification in Cuba, that process can be expected to generate inflationary pressures and disequilibria in the balance of payments. Managing those effects can take time, making it advisable to be able to count on alternative sources of financing in the multilateral arena and on knowledge of the institutions.

At the same time, the financing provided by multilateral development banks is insufficient in relation to the growing needs of nations—yet to lack those institutions would be more traumatic. Thus, these IFIs should be viewed as alternatives that may complement domestic efforts to finance development; by the nature of their funding, they offer benefits in terms of the cost of financing, building capacity, and channeling technical and financial resources. Cuba cannot continue to ignore those opportunities. Beyond the financing, these institutions' activities have been shown to have a counter-cyclical character, which is particularly important for small and mid-sized economies, especially in a context characterized by an accentuated cyclical tendency in external capital flows.

However, the issue remains politically sensitive for Cuba. There is still a degree of resistance to change that hampers attempts to give priority to this chapter's topic in the short run. There is also a lack of knowledge about the role played by international financial institutions at the global level and of the potential opportunities that could be derived from ties with them.

Anticipating a context that is sure to come will be the key to success. What matters is for Cuba to be capable of successfully linking its strategic development objectives, priorities, and urgent short-run needs with the possibilities offered by the multilateral institutions.

Bibliography

Banco Mundial. 2017a. Cartera de Proyectos por países, China. http://projects.bancomundial.org/search?lang=es&searchTerm=&countrycode_exact=CN.

———. 2017b. Cartera de Proyectos por países, Vietnam. http://projects.bancomundial.org/search?lang=es&searchTerm=&countrycode_exact=VN.

———. 2017c. Cartera de Proyectos por países, Rusia. http://projects.bancomundial.org/search?lang=es&searchTerm=&countrycode_exact=RU.

Buira, Ariel. 2003. "An Analysis of IMF Conditionality." Paper prepared for the XVI Technical Group Meeting of the Intergovernmental Group of 24. Port of Spain, Trinidad and Tobago. February 13–14, pp. 1–35.

Feinberg, Richard E. 2011. "Extender la mano: la nueva economía de Cuba y la respuesta internacional. Iniciativa para las Américas." Brookings Institution. November. https://www.brookings.edu/wp.../1118_cuba_feinberg_spanish.pdf.

———. 2012a. "The International Financial Institutions and Cuba: Relations with Non-member States." In Association for the Study of the Cuban Economy, *Cuba in Transition* 22: 44–59.

———. 2012b. "Cuba y las Instituciones Financieras Internacionales," *Revista Temas, Catalejo*. January 17.

García Lorenzo, Tania. "Acerca de la propuesta sobre la incorporación de Cuba al IMF," *Revista Temas, Catalejo*. January 17.

Griffiths, Jesse, and Konstantinos Todoulos. 2014. *Conditionally Yours. An Analysis of the Policy Conditions Attached to IMF Loans*, pp. 1–20. Brussels: Eurodad.

Helms-Burton. 1996. "Cuban Liberty and Democratic Solidarity (Libertad) Act of 1996, 104–114, p. 12.

IMF. 2002. "Guidelines on Conditionality. Prepared by the Legal and Policy Development and Review Departments (In consultation with other departments). Approved by Timothy F. Geithner and François Gianviti, September 25, 2002," pp. 1–11.

———. 2010. "Caribbean Regional Technical Assistance Center (CARTAC)." Program Document. Washington DC.

———. 2011. "Convenio Constitutivo del Fondo Monetario Internacional (1944)." Traducción de la Sección de español y portugués, Departamento de Tecnología y Servicios Generales del IMF. pp. 5–7, 24–27.

———. 2016a. "China: Financial Position in the Fund as of December 31, 2016." www.imf.org.

———. 2016b. "Viet Nam. Financial Position in the Fund as of December 31, 2016." www.imf.org.

———. 2016c. "Russia. Financial Position in the Fund as of December 31, 2016." www.imf.org.

Leckow, Ross. 2002. "Conditionality in the International Monetary Fund," pp. 1–8. Washington: IMF.

Monreal, Pedro. 2015. "Cuba y el IMF: ¿Qué podemos aprender de Stiglitz, de China y de Islandia?" In *Cuba Posible, Proyecto del Centro Cristiano de Reflexión y Diálogo-Cuba*, 17 December: 1–9.

Partido Comunista de Cuba. 2016. "Conceptualización del modelo económico y social cubano de desarrollo socialista. Plan nacional de desarrollo económico y social hasta 2030: propuesta de visión de la nación, ejes y sectores estratégicos." Havana: Seventh Congress of the Communist Party of Cuba, tabloid, 6 June.

Pérez, Lorenzo. 2012. "Comment: Cuba and the International Financial Institutions." In Association for the Study of the Cuban Economy, *Cuba in Transition* 22: 75–77.

———. 2016. "Mirando al IMF desde adentro: apuntes sobre la necesaria entrada de Cuba." In *Cuba Posible, Proyecto del Centro Cristiano de Reflexión y Diálogo-Cuba*, 16 January.

Pujol, Joaquin. 1991. "Membership Requirements in the IMF: Possible Implications for Cuba." Paper presented at the First Annual Meeting of the Association for the Study of the Cuban Economy, Miami, 16 August. www.ascecuba.org/c /wp-content/uploads/2014/09/v01-pujol.pdf.

———. 2012. "Cuba's Membership in the IMF and Other International Financial Institutions and Their Possible Role in Promoting Sustainable Economic Growth in Cuba." In Association for the Study of the Cuban Economy, *Cuba in Transition* 22: 60–72.

Rodríguez José Luis. 2015. "El proceso de transformaciones económicas en Cuba y el IMF." In *Cuba Posible. Proyecto del Centro Cristiano de Reflexión y Diálogo-Cuba* (Sección: ¿Debe de entrar Cuba en el IMF?), 30 November: 9–13.

United Nations, Economic and Social Council. 2015. "Transforming Our World: the 2030 Agenda for Sustainable Development," finalized text for adoption, 1 August, pp. 11–22.

Vidal, Pavel. "La reintegración económica de Cuba: ¿Debemos unirnos a las instituciones financieras internacionales?" In *Cuba Posible. Proyecto del Centro Cristiano de Reflexión y Diálogo-Cuba* (Sección: ¿Debe de entrar Cuba en el IMF?), 30 November: 2–8.

9

The Availability and Quality of Data on Cuban Economic Development: Implications for Policy and Empirical Research

Lorena G. Barberia

In this volume, distinguished Cuban economists examine Cuba's economic performance and policies from the beginning of Raúl Castro's administration to the end of 2016. They show that there is continuity with the reforms instituted by the government of Fidel Castro and that gradualism continues to mark the pace of reform. Important changes have been introduced to economic policies since Raúl Castro assumed the presidency of Cuba in 2006, but the structural challenges facing the Cuban economy remain significant. Parliamentary elections will be held in Cuba in 2018. Raúl Castro will not seek a new term as president; the National Assembly of People's Power Assembly will elect a new president. The administration that assumes office will inherit a difficult situation. These problems include:

- GDP growth is stable but stagnant, averaging 1.6% from 2007 to 2016.
- Fiscal policy balances are fragile; short-term external debt obligations are increasing and fiscal deficits are mounting.
- Efforts toward a unified exchange rate have been unsuccessful and the distortions caused by multiple exchange rates and markets are exacerbating growing inequalities.
- The limited growth of exports, tourism and FDI combined with a high level of imports continue to exert pressures on Cuba's balance of payments.
- While the state and state enterprises continue to dominate the economy, their capacity to generate jobs and undertake investments is limited.
- Cooperatives (agricultural and non-agricultural) and the self-employed have become important growth pillars, but their potential to generate infrastructure and employment are limited.

- Almost 20 years ago, the last official public estimate showed one in five Cuban households "at risk" of poverty. With lackluster economic performance, there are few reasons to believe that these figures have improved.

To address these challenges, the next administration will necessarily turn to evaluations of Cuban development policies based on the careful analysis of Cuban macroeconomic data. A noteworthy issue that should not be avoided in these discussions is whether the data needed to understand Cuba's development trajectory are reliable. In this short reflection, I argue and provide empirical evidence to show that the data used to assess Cuban development are flawed.

This issue has consistently been raised as a concern in the scholarship on Cuban economic development, including in the research published by Harvard University's David Rockefeller Center for Latin American Studies (DRCLAS) since the early 2000s (Domínguez, et al. 2004, Domínguez, et al. 2012, Domínguez, et al. 2017). As the chapters in the current volume underscore and as I will further argue below, in recent years there has been a marked increase in the public reporting of data by Cuba's official government agencies, including the national statistical agency, the *Oficina Nacional de Estadística e Información* (ONEI). These improvements are especially noteworthy, as the government of Raúl Castro has actively chosen to improve the disclosure of data in a context of adversity and economic stagnation.

At the same time, the availability of the primary data has been limited; researchers have constrained access to data and to the methodologies used to calculate economic indicators. Furthermore, there are still major concerns with the quality of available data in light of the issues discussed in this volume. To illustrate these concerns, I focus on the problems with respect to the measurement of national income and economic growth. A second issue is that some statistics that were scarce in the early 1990s have altogether disappeared from official reports. The most prominent examples are the vanishing of the reporting of income received from remittances, which is a standard indicator that most governments include in balance of payment statistics, and the percentage of the neediest Cuban households based on household survey data.

My focus in drawing attention to the data quality of Cuban statistics is not meant as a criticism of the contributions in this volume. On the contrary, the little we do know is precisely due to the exceptional efforts of scholars who persist in their efforts to produce noteworthy contributions under severe data constraints. However, we must recognize that Cuba's data deficiencies are significant and make research on Cuban development less robust. Moreover, poor statistics and incorrect statistical inferences matter for policy; they lead actors such as policymakers, entrepreneurs and managers to choose less effective or altogether less beneficial policies. In this chapter, I briefly discuss some of the major data issues for Cuba and their implications for development research, and address some strategies that one can undertake to reduce these biases.

Data Quality

Gross Domestic Product (GDP) indicators are one of the most widely used measures to assess economic well-being and often used in comparative analysis across countries and across time. Despite the significant efforts made to standardize protocols to calculate national income, significant difficulties in the reliability, or consistency, of this indicator remain (Jerven 2013). In the case of most countries, the standard approach to measure GDP is to sum the value added of the production of goods and services in all sectors of the economy. To standardize comparison, a base year is selected and GDP in other years is calculated relative to this base year. In addition to this method, GDP can also be calculated as the sum of the incomes (wages, rent, profits) or the sum of all expenditures (consumption, investment, government, and the trade balance). In theory, all three methodologies should yield the same results, and to be more reliable, governments typically report GDP based on different methodologies as a means of guaranteeing measurement validity. In practice, however, some methods are less appropriate than others for capturing specific sectors of the economy. For example, GDP calculations based on expenditures tend to measure private consumption poorly (Jerven 2013).

The proper measurement of any economic indicator, as Vishwanath and Kaufmann 2001 affirm more generally, requires that "the criteria and methodologies used for gathering and interpreting information, as well as any changes in methodologies, should be fully disclosed to prevent deliberate withholding or distortion of information." In the case of Cuban GDP calculations, the ONEI (2016) statistical yearbook has considerably improved the details provided regarding the criteria utilized to calculate national income. However, given the characteristics of the Cuban economy, there are several reasons to suspect the existence of significant measurement error of GDP. The chapters in this volume help us to understand why. Consider five factors that complicate Cuban GDP estimates and their reliability.

First, as Torres carefully highlights in his chapter in this volume, many different markets operate simultaneously in Cuba. As these differ according to pricing mechanisms (regulated, fixed, or free-market) and the type of currency (CUP, CUC, USD), more precise GDP calculations necessarily require making assumptions about how to assess the contribution of different sectors to national income; these in turn depend on assumptions of which values to use for each currency. However, the statistical appendix provided by ONEI does not disclose how it arrives at these GDP calculations. This is a problem for understanding present-day Cuba economic performance, but the hope is that this obstacle will be eliminated in the short to medium term, especially if the process of unifying the existing multiple exchange rate system is completed, thereby making statistical calculations of GDP much easier.

Second, Cuban statistical yearbooks only publish GDP figures in constant prices in CUPs. This is helpful because GDP figures in nominal terms would offer only limited insight; to be more useful, nominal gains in income must be corrected for inflation, hence constant prices. However, in order to obtain real GDP growth, we would need a CPI index that adjusts for the prices of the consumer basket, taking into account the rate of inflation in the different currencies that operate within the domestic economy. Unfortunately, however, ONIE only reports a CPI for CUP-denominated prices. If this is the only indicator used to convert GDP to constant prices, there are reasons to be concerned about the calculation. Moreover, as Torres reports in Table 2 of his chapter, official estimates of inflation in peso-denominated currency are quite low (an average 1.58 between 2007 and 2016). If so, then Cuban inflation rates were lower than in the United States (where the average was 1.92% in the same period), but higher than in Japan (where the average was 1.29%) (Organization for Economic Co-operation and Development 2016).

Third, official Cuban GDP figures are reported in constant 1997 CUP prices. The selection of the base year of 1997 most likely also contributes to mismeasurement of GDP figures. As Jerven (2013) underscores, the selection of the base year is important in appropriately measuring GDP because the base year determines the year for which the prices used for accounting are held constant and for which the weight of each sector was calculated. Given that the statistical appendix does not carefully elaborate on the weighting methodology in the base year and the adjustments that have been made to update the base year, it is difficult to evaluate the validity of this base year nearly 20 years later. However, in an economy such as Cuba's, which is undergoing significant transformation with the rise of an important non-state sector during the 2010s, as Pérez Villanueva discusses in his chapter, it is likely that 1997 weights are no longer appropriate.

Fourth, there are important asymmetries between GDP data and trends in other macroeconomic indicators, which run contrary to conventional economic expectations. For example, one cannot help but be perplexed by the asymmetries between GDP growth and unemployment between 2007 and 2015 as depicted by Figure 1 (based on the official data reported by Torres in this volume). After a period of economic contraction in 2008–9, the Cuban economy began to recover in the subsequent years with growth peaking at 3.2% in 2011, yet unemployment continued to soar steadily, peaking at 4.6% in 2012. In 2012, the economy began to decelerate, but unemployment fell. While unemployment may be lagging GDP trends, there may be other reasons for this disparity, including the relation between formal and informal markets, but these hypotheses are difficult to test and verify with existing statistical data.

Figure 9.1: GDP Growth and Unemployment, 2007–2016

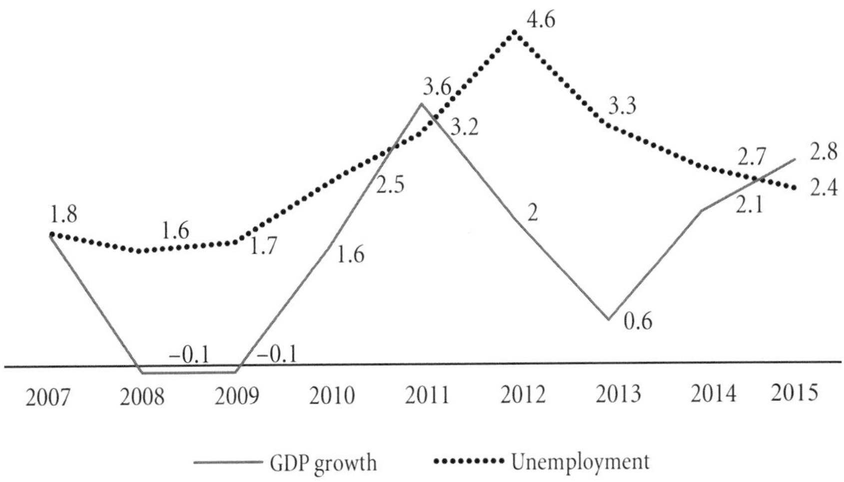

Source: Torres (2017)

Finally, there is an emerging and robust scholarship showing that the production and dissemination of economic data systematically vary. As Hollyer, Rosendorff and Vreeland (2014) document, even governments with comparatively more transparent data reputations strategically release, replace and withdraw data. Statistical events are often driven by politics. An excellent example is described by Rawski (2001), who illustrates how policy reforms affected the formulation of Chinese economic data during the transition of its centrally planned economy to one that is more open and market-oriented.

After Beijing established the objective of 8% annual growth as a "great political responsibility," China's provinces, main cities, and regions reported an average growth rate of 9.72% in 1998. The Chinese national statistical bureau, however, reported the national growth rate as 7.8%. For Rawski (2001), the data provide evidence that there are statistical problems at both the local and national levels. Local governments are pressured to inflate data, as they are held accountable for meeting targets. However, Chinese national indicators for growth rate are also suspiciously close to government targets. This is questionable because other indicators in the same statistical report suggest that there was a downturn in economic activity in 1998. For example, energy consumption fell 1.7% in the same period. Although it is possible that a portion of this decrease is due to increased efficiencies in energy use, Rawski argues that this indicator correlates strongly with GDP growth.

For these reasons, Rawski (2001) proposes that corrections must be made in both local and national statistics for China in 1998. Basing himself on an alternative calculation still using official data, he estimates that China's economy grew at a rate of 5.7%, though he is very careful to recognize that this estimate continues to be plagued by measurement error and biases. An interesting footnote to this example bears mention. Because of his work, Rawski was hired as a consulting expert by the Chinese National Statistical Bureau and has contributed to the improvement of Chinese statistical analysis.

Data Availability and Coverage

Data availability and data sources determine the quality of statistics. If data are not available, very limited research can be undertaken on important subjects for students of development, concerned decision makers, and economic actors. This is strikingly apparent in examining scholarship on Cuba's development challenges. Here, I turn to two issues—the measurement of poverty and remittances—which are closely connected to the issues in this volume, but underexplored in large part because social science research on these topics has progressed very slowly due to data limitations (Barberia 2017).

There has been a marked increase in Cuban families living in conditions of economic duress and in the wealth gaps between Cubans (Espina Prieto 2004, Domínguez, et al. 2017). However, as the pressure of these changes has magnified, the statistics mapping these dynamics, which were scarcely available in the early 1990s, have disappeared altogether from official statistical publications. In the late 1990s the National Institute of Economic Research (INIE) began reporting the proportion of the urban population characterized as being "at-risk of not meeting basic needs" and the Gini coefficient. The data, based on nationally representative samples of surveys of households, helped scholars and officials to understand Cuban society from a year prior to the fall of the Soviet bloc, 1989, until 1999. Similar to poverty measures normally employed to gauge unmet needs, Ferriol (1999) calculated the "at risk population" based on the percentage of the population unable to meet a minimum level of consumption. Almost three-fourths of Cuba's population was considered to be urban in that period, according to Cuban population statistics (ONEI (Oficina Nacional de Estadísticas) 2016). The share of the "at-risk population" more than doubled in eight years, so that by 1996 approximately 15% of Cuban households living in urban areas could be considered to fit that category. Three years later, in 1999, the at-risk of poverty share of the population increased by a further 33%. Thus, by 1999, one in five households (20%) were estimated to be part of an at-risk population.

Since 1999, however, further studies on Cuba's household earnings and expenditures, based on nationally representative household surveys, have either not been conducted or not been made publically available. As a result, the number of studies focused on examining poverty and inequality dynamics have decreased, and those that have been published have based their findings on sub-optimal sampling techniques for a restricted geographical region and time period (Barberia 2017).

Starting in the 1990s, Cuba also experienced an unprecedented surge in remittances. These material resources sent to Cuban households from abroad quickly became the largest type of international financial inflow, entering Cuba at a rapid and increasing pace (Barberia 2004). Three decades after the collapse of the Soviet bloc and Cuba's insertion into the world economy, remittances remain larger than either capital inflows or official development assistance. These flows of remittances strongly affected the well-being of thousands of Cuban households.

Official Cuban government statistics report remittances as a part of "net current transfers." In principle, this follows standard practices followed by the International Monetary Fund (IMF), in which international balance of payments statistics include remittances under this same line item. In practice, however, there are no meaningful, continuous data on remittance flows to Cuba for most of the 21st century; even net current transfers have not been reported in Cuba's balance of payment statistics since 2009 (ONEI 2015).[1] Likewise, there are no micro-level studies to elucidate macro-estimations of remittances flows. This is because there are no further publicly available studies for Cuba based on nationally representative household surveys that include published information on all sources of household earnings.

How to Reduce or Mitigate the Problems

Problems associated with the quality of macro-economic statistics are not unique to Cuba. The complexity of statistical measurement is an enormous and costly undertaking for most governments; there are ongoing discussions in every country about how to improve current estimates learning from past mistakes. Alas, United Nations world population estimates were revised 17 times from 1951 to 1996. Today, as a result of better data measurement efforts, we know that these projections still failed to account for 20% of the world's population (Cooper and Layard 2002).

In recent years, scholars have paid increasing attention to government collection and dissemination of aggregate economic data (Vishwanath and Kaufmann 2001, Adsera, et al. 2003, Hollyer, et al. 2014). The magnitude of this problem for countries in Sub-Saharan Africa (Jerven 2013) and China (Rawski 2001) has been documented in important volumes. More generally, the poor quality of government data has been discussed with respect to fiscal policy in developed and developing economies (De Renzio and Masud 2011). On the basis of an analysis of data published in 2010 covering 94 countries, De Renzio and Masud (2011) conclude, "the state of budget transparency around the world is poor." These problems also pertain to many well-accepted data sources that academics and policymakers commonly use, including the International Monetary Fund (IMF)'s primary statistical publications, the *International Financial Statistics* and the *Government Finance Statistics*, both of which are replete with data for the same indicator for the same year but do not match in books from different years of the same publication.

To circumvent these difficulties, researchers and governments increasingly turn to innovative methodologies that take advantage of data that do exist, but perhaps have been underexploited. This potential has yet to be applied to Cuba, but its next administration or a group of scholars may replicate these techniques to produce meaningful data for Cuba. Here I provide one example, again focusing on GDP, because it is a vital area where Cuba's next administration surely will need further data to help guide decision-making.

Given the ongoing difficulties with measuring economic growth especially in developing countries, Henderson, Storeygard, and Weil (2012) use data on night lights (satellite imagery from outer space) to estimate economic activity for 188 countries between 1992 and 2008. The authors postulate that night lights are a proxy for economic activity, as consumption and investment activities in the evening or night require electricity. They show that the intensity of night lights and its growth over time correlate strongly with the intensity of economic activity (or economic growth).

Using the data provided by Henderson, Storeygard, and Weil (2012), Figure 2 shows average annual economic activity between 1992 and 2008 for Cuba as measured using night light activity. Several caveats are in order. First, the data do not cover the specific period analyzed in this volume (2007–2016). Second, we should not expect GDP growth and night light activity to match economic output perfectly, as elasticities are not equal. Finally, electricity provision in Cuba is heavily subsidized and managed by the state. Notwithstanding these caveats, the data offer several interesting insights.

Figure 9.2: Cuban GDP Evaluation Using Night Light Activity, 1992–2008

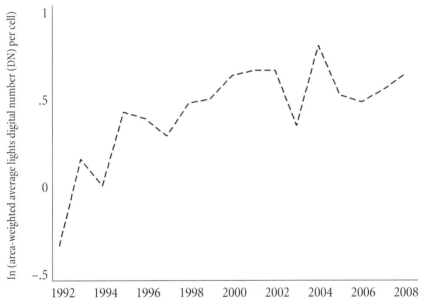

Source: Henderson, Storeygard, and Weil (2012)

The purpose of this example is not to analyze this series in depth, but merely to point out that this type of data could be further analyzed and used to compare with GDP performance. Moreover, given the specificity of the data that is being collected by satellites on night activity, this type of data could be even more useful for examining inequalities across provinces and even smaller micro-regions (in the city of Havana, for example). Henderson, Storeygard, and Weil (2012) undertake this exercise for sub-Saharan Africa. Their findings run counter to those of the economic development scholars who have long argued that there are advantages for populations more closely located to the coast. Between 1992 and 2008, during a period of rapidly growing trade, they show that coastal areas in Africa grew more slowly than interior areas.

Conclusion

The data quality and availability problems affecting Cuban development research are too large to dismiss. For many years, researchers have continued to rely on poor quality data given the constraints listed above. As I have argued in this brief chapter concluding this volume, policymakers and researchers continue to make costly mistakes when they use existing data on Cuba.

Note

1. For 2009 and earlier, one can attempt to estimate international migrants' remittances for Cuba by calculating the difference between net current transfers and official development assistance. As neither of these items is reported separately in any statistical publication in Cuba, one could try to use data reported in the World Bank's World Development Indicators (WDI) for the latter. For significant periods, however, the data for official development assistance are not available from the WDI database for Cuba.

References

Adsera, Alicia, Carles Boix, and Mark Payne. 2003. "Are You Being Served? Political Accountability and Quality of Government." *The Journal of Law, Economics, and Organization* 19: 445–90.

Barberia, Lorena. 2004. "Remittances to Cuba: An Evaluation of Cuban and U.S. Government Policy Measures." In *The Cuban Economy at the Start of the Twenty-First Century*, eds. Jorge I. Domínguez, Omar Everleny Pérez Villanueva and Lorena Barberia. Cambridge, Mass.: Harvard University David Rockefeller Center for Latin American Studies ; Distributed by Harvard University Press. 319–53.

Barberia, Lorena G. 2017. "The Impact of Remittances on Poverty and Inequality for Cuba: Lessons from Latin America." In *Social Policies and Decentralization in Cuba: Change in the Context of 21st-Century Latin America*, eds. Jorge I. Domínguez, Maria del Carmen Zabala Arguelles, Mayra Espina Prieto and Lorena G. Barberia. Cambridge, MA: David Rockefeller Center for Latin American Studies, Harvard University Press.

Cooper, Richard N., and Richard Layard. 2002. *What the Future Holds: Insights from Social Science.* Cambridge, Mass.: Harvard University Press.

De Renzio, Paolo, and Harika Masud. 2011. "Measuring and Promoting Budget Transparency: The Open Budget Index as a Research and Advocacy Tool." *Governance* 24: 607–16.

Domínguez, Jorge I., Maria del Carmen Zabala Arguelles, Mayra Espina Prieto, and Lorena G. Barberia, eds. 2017. *Social Policies and Decentralization in Cuba: Change in the Context of 21st-Century Latin America.* Cambridge, MA: David Rockefeller Center for Latin American Studies, Harvard University Press.

Domínguez, Jorge I., Omar Everleny Pérez Villanueva, and Lorena Barberia. 2004. *The Cuban Economy at the Start of the Twenty-First Century*, David Rockefeller Center Series on Latin American Studies, Harvard University ; 13th. Cambridge, Mass.: Harvard University David Rockefeller Center for Latin American Studies ; Distributed by Harvard University Press.

Domínguez, Jorge I., Omar Everleny Pérez Villanueva, Mayra Espina Prieto, and Lorena Barberia. 2012. *Cuban Economic and Social Development: Policy Reforms and Challenges in the 21st Century* David Rockefeller Center Series on Latin American Studies, Harvard University. Cambridge, Mass.: Harvard University David Rockefeller Center for Latin American Studies ; Distributed by Harvard University Press.

Espina Prieto, Mayra Paula. 2004. "Social Effects of Economic Adjustment: Equality, Inequality and Trends Toward Greater Complexity in Cuban Society." In *The Cuban Economy at the Start of the Twenty First Century*, ed. Omar Everleny Pérez Villanueva Jorge I. Domínguez, Mayra Espina Prieto and Lorena Barberia. Cambridge: Mass.: David Rockefeller Center, Harvard University Press. 209–44.

Henderson, J. Vernon, Adam Storeygard, and David N. Weil. 2012. "Measuring Economic Growth from Outer Space." *American Economic Review* 102: 994–1028.

Hollyer, James R., B. Peter Rosendorff, and James Raymond Vreeland. 2014. "Measuring Transparency." *Political Analysis* 22: 413–34.

Jerven, Morten. 2013. *Poor Numbers: How We Are Misled by African Development Statistics and What to Do About It.* Ithaca, NY: Cornel University Press.

ONEI (Oficina Nacional de Estadísticas). 2016. *Anuario Estadístico De Cuba 2015.* Havana: ONEI.

Organization for Economic Co-operation and Development. 2016. *Main Economic Indicators* Geneva: OECD.

Rawski, Thomas G. 2001. "China by the Numbers: How Reform Has Affected China's Economic Statistics." *China Perspectives*: 25–34.

Vishwanath, Tara, and Daniel Kaufmann. 2001. "Toward Transparency." *World Bank Research Observer* 16: 41–58.